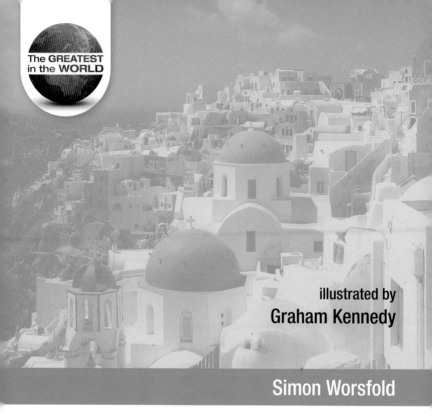

The GREATEST
in the WORLD

illustrated by
Graham Kennedy

Simon Worsfold

The Greatest

Travel

Tips in the World

A 'The Greatest in the World' book

www.thegreatestintheworld.com

Illustrations:
Graham Kennedy
gkillus@aol.com

Cover & layout design:
the designcouch
www.designcouch.co.uk

Cover images:
© Sascha Burkard; © Marius Jasaitis; © Lorelyn Medina;
© Stephen Strathdee
all courtesy of www.fotolia.com

Copy editor:
Bronwyn Robertson
www.theartsva.com

Series creator/editor:
Steve Brookes

First published in 2007 by Public Eye Publications

This edition published in 2007 by
The Greatest in the World Ltd., PO Box 3182
Stratford-upon-Avon, Warwickshire CV37 7XW

Text and illustrations copyright © 2007 – The Greatest in the World Ltd.

A CIP catalogue record for this book is available from the British Library
ISBN 978-1-905151-73-8

Printed and bound in China by 1010 Printing International Ltd.

Dedicated to my loving wife Breege,
my family and all the people I've met
on my travels who have shown me what
a wonderful world we have and how
important it is we save it for the future.

Contents

Introduction

In the first tourism job I had, running a sunny campsite on the shores of Lake Garda in northern Italy, the first thing my boss told me was that people on holiday always forget to pack their brain. Knowing that campers were about the most resourceful holidaymakers going, I thought this was a bit harsh. You could usually rely on them to build an emergency guy rope out of little more than twigs and grass.

But I didn't begrudge my boss's intolerant attitude and discarded his advice as the words of a man jaded by years of waiting on other people when really, all he wanted was for other people to wait on him. To my alarm, however, as we crept towards peak season, I began to see what he meant.

By July the campsite was full from car park to swimming pool and I found myself surrounded by campers from all over Western Europe – Holland, Germany, Italy, Austria and Britain whon to my surprise, needed more hand holding than most children on their first day at school. They would ask me things like: *Do you have a spare tent for my dog? Is it possible to get breakfast in bed?* And the season's classic: *Is that lake safe to swim in? I'm worried about sea snakes.*

I was in stitches. What on earth would make a person believe that sea snakes could possibly inhabit a mountain lake? Or that a campsite manager (who was in reality little more than a glorified toilet cleaner) would be offering an on-demand catering service!

And then it hit me. These people had not forgotten to pack brains at all. It was all part of the plan. Even for campers, switching off was the luxury of their holiday. And it makes sense. It was what they were paying for, at the end of the day. Because when you've worked so hard to earn it, time off is sacred; and nothing gets in the way of a good holiday. Not even the old noggin!

But this experience also made me realise, on my own travels years later, that you must not let the pleasure you get from disengaging, at best, cause you to miss out on something, or, at worst, leave you at risk. Once in South Africa I took a shortcut through a serene, sandy woodland to discover later it was known locally as Puff Adder Alley on account of the large snake population living there. Puff adders are aggressive: responsible for more deaths in Africa each year than almost any other kind, even the black mamba.

There are two things that make travel unique in our lives. One is how quickly you can find yourself out of your depth. The other is how much you can learn about yourself and the world if you are willing to push your limits and keep your wits about you. Hence The Greatest Travel Tips in the World: not a cultural crash course or an in depth city guide, but a book that will equip you for any trip you dare to plan. Whether you're visiting the relatives in Richmond or packing off to the cloud forests of Costa Rica, once you've read it, consider your brain packed.

Bon voyage!

Top Lists

"We wander
for distraction,
but we travel
for fulfilment.

Hilaire Belloc

chapter 1
Booking your holiday

Enjoy it!

The first rule of travel is: enjoy it. As many wise people have said, happiness is a journey, not a destination; so whether you're preparing for the big trip or you're en route already, sit back and soak it up. Seeing the world is a privilege and by appreciating it from the moment you book, you'll make more of the holiday itself.

A fresh start

Following the 'change is as good as a rest' mantra, many tour operators now offer specialist trips to revolutionise your life. Not just so you can come home with a new nose but to help you give up smoking or even learn to paint. Think about the change you'd like to make and type it into an Internet search engine next to the word holiday to see what comes up.

What do you want?

Before you book, think about what you want to get out of your holiday. Are you looking for relaxation? Excitement? To meet someone? The answer will help you choose the right kind of break. If you're travelling in a group, it is even more important to find out what everyone wants beforehand so you can all have a good time.

Party animal

We all hate to miss a good party, but imagine starting your holiday to discover you missed the country's biggest festival only a few days before. To find out what's going on where you're going to be, use **www.earthcalendar.net** or **www.whatsonwhen.com** to plan your next trip. What is Rio without the carnival, after all?

Take the temperature

Like an Aussie cooking a 'barbie' on the beach in the middle of December, remember it's not always cold at Christmas! If you're expecting a holiday of cool fresh air you don't want to arrive in the middle of a heat wave (or vice versa), so use a world weather guide like Fodor's, **www.worldclimate.com** or **www.worldweather.org** to make sure you get the weather you had in mind.

Sporting journeys

International sports events like the football World Cup always bring out the best in the host country and this makes it a fantastic time to visit, even if you don't have tickets for the games. You'll need to book ahead but there are many specialist tour operators out there providing itineraries for everything from 'Barmy Army' cricket tours to the traditional 'Naadam' Olympics in Mongolia.

Travel to train

If you're into sport, another good use of a holiday can be to spend the time raising your game. At one end of the scale you might just fancy a week of golf on the Algarve but at the other end, athletes can use their 'time off' to take their training to the next level.

Stuck for ideas?

If you're not a regular newspaper or travel magazine reader, another good place for holiday ideas is a travel show. They are attended by hundreds of tour operators offering just about every type of holiday imaginable. Many also run special offers just for the show so you might be able to bag a bargain to boot.

Package or DIY?

The internet hasn't brought an end to the package holiday but it has given us a lot more flexibility. If you 'do it yourself' by booking your flights and accommodation separately, it's a good idea to book two different hotels for the first night and cancel one as soon as you know you've got a good room. Hotels have been known to give away booked rooms to people without reservations just to be sure they get the business on the day. For you, a cancellation fee is better than being left on the streets on the first night of your holiday.

The World is
a book, and those
who do not travel
read only a page.

St. Augustine

Bargain basement

There are some great deals out there and with more people flying than ever before, the non-environmentalists among us would say we've been in a 'golden age' of cheap airline travel recently. How long this continues remains to be seen, but for now remember, the bigger the discount the greater the restrictions, so don't expect a refund if you have to cancel, and do expect to be getting up very early for the flight.

Save paper, time and money

Many tour operators now make their brochures available online. This not only saves paper and time, but could even help to hold down the price of your holiday in future. Travel brochures might be free to you, but they are expensive to print and at the end of the day, that's all factored into the cost of your holiday. To save you having to search through hundreds of websites for the right brochure, go straight to **www.brochurebank.co.uk**.

Be inspired

There are many good travel magazines and websites with inspiration for your next trip, but for more up front reviews about the places you're thinking of visiting use internet forums like Lonely Planet's 'Thorn Tree' (**www.lonelyplanet.co.uk**) or Holiday Watchdog (**www.holidaywatchdog.com**) to read reviews written by people who haven't been paid to go there.

Confirm your flight

With every flight, but especially when buying online, always call the airline a day or two before you fly to confirm your booking has gone through and that they are expecting you. It's also worth checking that you have a seat allocation because if you don't and your flight is overbooked, you could be the one left on the tarmac.

Arriving safely

If you're travelling alone or with young children, try to avoid booking a flight that arrives in the middle of the night because it will leave you tired and more vulnerable during the first few hours in the country. If you can't avoid arriving in the middle of the night, arrange for a representative from your hotel to come and meet you at the airport.

Top 10

far out holidays

1 Cycling through the tropical jungles of Guatemala and Honduras.

2 Staying in an ice hotel above the Arctic Circle in Sweden.

3 Riding the Trans-Mongolian Railway from Moscow to Beijing.

4 Sleeping underground in a cave hotel in Spain.

5 Learning to cook on a residential course in Thailand.

6 Diving with whale sharks off Ningaloo Reef in Western Australia.

7 Sailing through the Arctic on an ice breaker cruise ship.

8 Getting high in the Brazilian Amazon in a treetop hotel.

9 Keeping dry in the deep in an underwater hotel in Florida.

10 Aligning your chakras on a yogic retreat in India.

chapter 2
Getting ready to go

Do your research

Knowing about your destination helps you choose the right holiday and keeps you safe when you get there. Travel Guides like Footprint and Lonely Planet are a great starting point, but to really get Inside a country ask your local bookstore for books written by people who who were born and bred there. They will give a lot more insight.

Get a second opinion

As well as reading up on what to do at your destination, it's also worth reading up on what not to do. For up-to-date safety advice, check a number of official sources like the British Foreign and Commonwealth Office website (see **www.fco.gov.uk** and go to the 'travel advice by country' section) and the U.S. Department of State (see **www.state.gov** and go to the 'travel warnings' section). They will give you the updates that didn't make it into the last edition of your travel guide.

Ditch the travel guide

Travel guides are best for choosing destinations, not hotels, so if you buy one make sure you read it before you fly. Try not to rely on it too much when you arrive either, as prices may be 10-20% higher than quoted and many of the hotels listed will be crowded with all the people who bought the same book! The best way to beat the crowds is to be a little adventurous and be open to recommendations from locals and tourists alike.

Pocket book

To get the best out of your travel guide, make notes on all the places you'd most like to visit before you go and take these with you instead of the entire book. That way, you can fit all the information you need into your pocket and, now that you're no longer tied to your travel 'bible', you're free to explore all the lesser known places it didn't tell you about.

Local know-how

Do you know what all tourist information has in common? It always paints a good picture of a place, never a bad one. This is great for selling holidays, but not so great at telling you about any potential risks of travelling there. The best sources of honest and up-to-date information are local newspapers. And thanks to the globalisation of English, most countries now have editions you can read. If available, it's worth buying a copy as soon as you arrive.

"When preparing to travel, lay out all your clothes and all your money. Then take half the clothes and twice the money.

Susan Heller

Travel light, travel far

This is the best piece of travel advice going. The heavier your bag is, the more hassle you're going to have carrying it. Before you leave home try walking a mile with your bag fully packed, then decide if you've packed enough stuff. As a rule of thumb, the longer you're away, the less you should take because you'll be washing your clothes regularly and you'll have more opportunities to buy souvenirs.

How to pack less

The key to packing less is to take a washing line and travel wash. How many times have you come home with unused clothes because you've just worn your favourite outfits night after night? When you can wash (and dry) your clothes on holiday, you get to wear your best gear whenever you want to and you don't have to pack as much in the first place.

How to pack smaller

If size is more important to you than weight, you can cram more gear into your bag by using a compressor like those made by Eagle Creek (**www.eaglecreek.com**). They work by squeezing all the air out of your clothes to make them smaller – though not lighter!

Mix and match

Efficient packing is all about mixing and matching your clothes. If all your tops match all your bottoms, you'll have less to carry and more outfits to wear. Try to avoid denim though as it's heavy and takes ages to dry if it gets wet.

What to take?

If you're stuck for ideas about what to take with you on holiday, there's a very handy website called the Universal Packing List (see **http://upl.codeq.info**) which suggests essential items for different trips depending on who's going where and when. It's a good idea to keep a note of what you've packed so you can check everything off the list when you leave the hotel and be certain you've left nothing behind.

Quick tip

TAKE A SMALLER BAG

If you are a habitual over-packer who comes home from every holiday with half a suitcase of clothes you never wore, think about taking a smaller bag on your next trip. It will force you to pack less and give your back and shoulders a break.

Compartmentalise

This is essential if you're moving about from place to place several times on your holiday. If you need your favourite shirt you don't want to have to unpack everything to get it, use stuff sacks (drawstring bags used for camping) or custom made packing cubes (available from most camping/travel stores) to separate your clothes into different compartments. They will save you a lot of hassle.

Clean toothbrush, cleaner teeth

To keep your toothbrush clean on holiday, always pack a toothbrush holder. Most encase them from top to tail but the best just cover the head and bristles. They are more lightweight and if you are super space-conscious, still allow you to cut the handle short.

Roll don't fold

When you're packing, try to roll soft cotton items like t-shirts and jeans instead of folding them. This not only reduces creasing but, in rounded luggage like backpacks and duffel bags, also saves space.

Bringing souvenirs home

When you travel it's worth packing an empty, lightweight bag just in case you go souvenir crazy and can't fit them all into your suitcase for the journey home. If you have a hard suitcase, you can use that to pack all the breakables padded by your clean clothes, and the soft bag for all your dirty washing.

To wheel or not to wheel?

Wheelie bags have become a bit of a hit in recent years and they're great on the smooth floors of an airport but can be a nightmare out on the roads. Dragging a bag with wheels around a city while it does a wrist-breaking 'R2D2 wobble' is a real pain. If you're going to be walking any distance, use a travel bag instead (see next tip). They're much easier to carry.

Take a day-pack

No holiday is complete without a day trip to see the sights, and it's really useful to have a small backpack with you for the camera and a few snacks. The best incorporate water bladders (made by companies like Platypus and Camelbak) so you can drink on the go.

Backpack or travel bag?

Purists will stand by their dual strap backpacks as the only way to go, but the more leisurely tourists among us will probably get more use out of a 'travel bag'. They combine the best aspects of a suitcase and backpack all in one – with both single and dual shoulder straps that smartly unzip from a panel on the back of the bag. This means you can hike with the best of them and still walk into a decent hotel without feeling like a backpacker. The other bonus is that you can check a travel bag into the hold of a plane without the straps getting damaged in transit.

Packing your valuables

Avoid packing valuables in your checked bags as they will be away from you for a long time on your journey, and might not be handled as carefully as you would like. It is best to keep your valuables on you at all times. If your luggage has outer pockets, never put anything delicate in them as it's unlikely to survive the journey.

Take miniatures

If you're only going away for a week or two, there's no need for family size bottles of shampoo. Instead, buy mini dispensers from your local chemist and fill them up from home with enough to last the trip. You can also get travel size toothpaste and even hairspray.

Buy it there

If you didn't pack it – don't panic; just buy it when you get there! In most places things are cheaper than they are at home and and make good souvenirs. Note that this doesn't apply to sun cream or camera accessories though as they're not always readily available and can be pricey.

Money talks

People say English is the global language but really it's numbers. '1, 2, 3' goes a lot further than 'one, two, three' so always pack a small calculator to help you through your price negotiations. You will always know how much you're being asked to pay and how much you're paying.

Holiday reading

A good book is essential on holiday but the last thing you want on the beach is a story about being eaten by sharks! The best holiday books reflect positively on the place you're visiting: like a novel set in a similar location or non-fiction that gives insight into the local way of life. Ask your bookstore for recommendations.

Top 10

travel items

1 Sarong.

2 Travel towel.

3 Head torch.

4 Calculator.

5 Aloe Vera gel.

6 A good book.

7 Waterproof stuff sack.

8 Flip flops.

9 Ear plugs.

10 Eye shades.

You scratch mine and I'll scratch yours

If you've got the sun cream, let your travel buddy take the after sun. You won't have as much to carry and there'll be no excuse for not getting a back rub every time you're in the sun!

Quick tip

KEEP IT DRY

Most luggage isn't waterproof and it is a nightmare to arrive at your hotel wearing two-day-old clothes to find everything soaking wet. Before you pack, line your luggage with a heavy duty bin liner or, if you have a backpack, buy a custom made waterproof cover from your local camping store.

Hands free

A head torch is one of the handiest items you can pack. It always shines where you need it and keeps your hands free at the same time: ideal for reading, finding your way back from the beach late at night, and packing for your return flight with the birds first thing in the morning.

Dirty washing

Always pack an empty bag to fill with dirty washing. Linen bags are lightweight, but not waterproof, while canvas bags are waterproof, but not lightweight; so the best option is to use a sealed, lightweight stuff sack (available from most camping stores) to hold damp items and keep the smell at bay.

Take a plug

Don't expect the hotel to supply one. If you can't wash or shave properly because the last tenant took the sink plug, it's the pits, especially after a long flight. Universal plugs are sold at most airports but you can always make your own by cutting a squash ball in half or, if you're travelling light, by buying a lemon when you arrive, cutting it in half and placing it over the plughole.

Download your sounds

If you haven't joined the music download revolution yet, you might want to before your next trip. There's no easier way to carry music with you. The players are light, hold loads of songs and will plug in almost anywhere. Two things to remember though: first, back-up all your music at home, and second, don't flash it about as an MP3 player is very attractive to thieves.

Plugging in

If you're travelling with a laptop and want to be able to connect to the Internet, take an acoustic coupler with you. This will connect your modem to most telephone lines and will get you online almost anywhere in the world.

Sarong

Another essential travel item – even for guys – is a sarong. It's great on the beach and doubles as a towel, scarf, pillow, pillowcase, tablecloth, shower wrap, toilet cubicle, and even a mobile changing room. It's also paper thin, lightweight, and dries in an instant.

Quick tip

BAG IT

Resealable food bags are a traveller's best friend. You can use them to stop your toiletries leaking, and with a few extra tucked away you'll be amazed at what other uses they have, from keeping your passport dry to packing wet swimming trunks.

Pillow

If a sarong doesn't quite cut it as a pillow for you and you're expecting some long journeys on your next trip, take a travel pillow with you as well. The smallest are inflatable but these are rarely the most comfortable. If you have room in your bag, a compressible pillow is better but my personal favourite is a reversible stuff sack with a fleece-lined interior. They are dual purpose and can be made to any size you want. Simply turn the bag inside out and fill it with soft, clean clothes.

Travel towel

How many times have you had to pack a beach towel while it was still wet? Or forgotten to pack it because it was still drying? Combined with a sarong to wrap around yourself, a travel towel is a much better option as it's smaller, more absorbent and dries much faster.

Shoe bag

You can't underestimate the value of a good shoe bag. You don't want to pack dirty shoes next to clean clothes and a zippable bag to keep them in is a good investment for any holiday. For extra protection, double wrap your shoes in a plastic bag.

Phone home

The cost of calling home varies a lot from one country to the next and rarely has much to do with the distance the call actually travels. For convenience, and so you always know you can afford to phone home, take a pre-paid calling card with you like those available from **www.globalcalling.com**. To find out how to get the best rate for calling home from your next destination, use **www.compare-phone-rates.com**.

Dog gone

If you have pets, make sure you visit the kennel or cattery before you drop them off there on the way to the airport to ensure you are happy with the facilities and the care they provide. You don't want your time off to be a misery for your loved one. If leaving them behind is too much, why not take your pet with you on holiday? With luxury pet hotels in Australia, a pet passport scheme in the EU, and guides like Pets Welcome giving specialist advice, it's never been easier.

chapter 3
Looking after your travel documents

How old is your passport?

You don't just need a passport to leave a country; you need one to get back in as well. Before you fly, check that yours doesn't expire while you're away. As a rule of thumb, you should never travel with less than six months' validity because this is an entry requirement in many countries. Some countries now require machine-readable passports so be sure that yours is modern enough to get you where you want to go.

Quick tip

DO YOU TAKE VISA?

It's not just restaurants that take Visa, Customs Officials do too. Find out well in advance what travel permits you need to visit a country as visas are almost impossible to obtain at short notice. In your capital city, contact the embassy or consulate of the country you will be visiting, or see their website for information.

> "If you actually look like your passport photo, you aren't well enough to travel.

Sir Vivian Fuchs

Stamp it out

If you pride yourself on the number of stamps in your passport, you'll probably also want to keep them neat and tidy and easy to read. Show me a customs official who cares about the presentation of your passport though, and I'll show you one who whistles while he works! To give them a little friendly guidance, put a rubber band across the pages between your photo and the next available visa page so it falls open exactly where they need it.

Applying for a visa

The ease of obtaining a visa depends on where you want to go and why. Some countries issue them the moment you arrive, while others require a lot of bureaucracy. If you have to go to the country's embassy in your capital city to apply for a visa in advance, make sure you have all the right documents, identification and photographs with you because there's no flexibility if you forget something. Note that journalists and those on business trips usually require non-tourist visas.

Take your receipts

One of the great advantages of booking online is that you can save money by paying for your flight and accommodation separately. But this also means you'll have more confirmations to remember. They are usually sent by email so check your junk/spam mailbox as well as your inbox, then print them out and staple them together. Check that each printout is clear because many airlines now use machine-readable barcodes for check-in.

Booking codes

Some airlines simply give you a booking code when you buy your tickets online and a good way to make sure you have this is to write it on a post-it note and attach it to the inside of your passport. When you arrive at the airport, punch the number into the self-service machine and away you go.

Security wallet

A security wallet is a pouch for your money and travel documents that can be worn around the neck, chest, waist, or leg. They're not always as secure as the name suggests, but they are useful for keeping everything in one place. They come in various shapes and sizes but whichever one you choose, make sure you keep it out of sight at all times as they are a magnet for thieves.

Hand in your departure card

If you have to complete a card on the airplane or in customs when you arrive at your destination (e.g. when flying to America from Britian), make sure you hand in the 'departure' section when you finally leave the country. If you fly home with this card, it goes on record that you never left the country and thus overstayed your visit. This is fine until you fly back to that country, at which point you will be detained until the matter is cleared up.

Home made security

To save money and make your travel documents even safer, sew a secret, internal pocket into an item of clothing like a pair of trousers or jacket so any would-be thief can't get their hands on your valuables.

Hiring a car?

If you want to drive away from your destination airport in a hire car, many countries require an International Driving Permit as well as your own. Your local driving agency will be able to tell you if you need one and where you can get it but even if it's not mandatory, it's a good idea to get one as they're printed in several languages and may help to smooth over any over-zealous officials you run into.

Wear and tear

If your passport becomes too worn or damaged you can have a lot of trouble in Customs and could even be refused entry. When you travel a lot it's worth investing in a durable cover to keep your passport neat and tidy. Some hotels give out complimentary branded passport covers to their guests, so to save a bit of cash, ask at the front desk next time you stay somewhere.

PHOTOCOPY EVERYTHING

Always carry photocopies of your passport photo page, visa, driving licence, insurance documents, air tickets, and credit or debit card when you travel, and keep them away from the originals in case you lose them. It's also a good idea to stash some cash (Sterling or U.S. Dollars) with the photocopies in case of an emergency.

Email to the rescue

To be extra safe, scan a copy of all your important documents (your passport photo page, visa, driving licence, air tickets, and credit and debit cards) into your computer and send the files as attachments to a web-based email account like **www.hotmail.com** or **www.gmail.com**. If you lose everything you can simply log on and print off what you need to get money and get home.

DID YOU KNOW?

The word atlas has only been associated with geography since the late sixteenth century when Rumold Mercator used a drawing of Atlas the Titan holding a globe above his shoulders as the frontispiece to his book of world maps. What's even more interesting about this is that Greek mythology makes no mention of this feat whatsoever: Atlas the Titan held up the heavens on his shoulders, not the earth.

Top 10

man-made travel Wonders of the World

1 Pyramids of Egypt (Gaza, near Cairo).

2 Great Wall of China (Northern China).

3 Taj Mahal (Agra, India).

4 Machu Picchu, Lost City of the Incas (Peru).

5 Bali Tropical Island (Indonesia).

6 Angkor Wat (Cambodia).

7 Forbidden City (Beijing, China).

8 Bagan Temples & Pagodas (Myanmar).

9 Karnak Temple (Egypt).

10 Teotihuacan (North of Mexico City).

GATE 11

DA J207
TO NEW YORK
DELAYED

chapter 4
Surviving the airport

Safe parking

There's no way round it, parking at airports costs a fortune and you're better off getting a lift from a friend. If you have to drive, leave the car in an official car park as cheaper, local alternatives have been known to 'use' or even 'lose' holidaymakers' cars while they're away. Wherever you leave it, make sure you park it yourself and take the keys with you.

Book in advance

Many airport parking facilities let you reserve a space in advance and might even give you a discount for doing so — especially if you book online. For the extra security and peace of mind, it's well worth the trouble. Contact your local airport authority for information.

Quick tip

FRUIT FLIES
Fruit is perfect plane food but be careful: many countries, like Chile and New Zealand, have strict quarantine controls that dole out hefty fines if you happen to walk through Customs carrying an illegal banana.

Go strapless

No matter what bag you have – suitcase, travelbag or backpack – always remove or secure the straps before you check it in so they don't get damaged in transit.

Getting through security

Tougher security means that check-in times are much longer than they used to be. On international flights, they can be up to three hours so leave plenty of time and check the road conditions beforehand. Wear socks as well as shoes because many airports will now scan passengers' shoes as well as their hand luggage. Finally, check with the airport or your airline for what you can and can't take with you, as fluctuating levels of security mean that restrictions can change without warning.

Checking in

If you booked your tickets online, you might be able to save time by checking in your own luggage at the airport, so don't forget your security password or barcode if you were issued one. One of the questions you will be asked is whether you packed the bags yourself so if you're carrying a bag for a friend, be sure you pack it with them and know what's inside. It's strictly prohibited to carry unknown items.

Unhappy birthday

If you're flying out to a celebration and have presents packed in your checked luggage, make sure they're not wrapped. If your bags are hand searched by security, they will unwrap them to check what's inside. Pack the paper, tape and ribbon separately.

Cosmetics

Be especially careful about what cosmetics you carry in your hand luggage. Increasingly, passengers are being restricted to carrying containers no larger than 100ml (especially through British airports), so pack anything larger than this in your checked luggage or you might have to leave it at the airport.

Getting the right seat

Many airlines now offer online check-in and if this is available, you should make your reservation as early as possible to get a good seat. To find out which is the best seat, use **www.seatguru.com** where the seats on most commercial airplanes are rated according to comfort. Be aware that even when you 'reserve' a seat online, the final allocation is only done when you check-in so always confirm with a member of staff when you get there. As a rule it's 'first come, first served' so if you must have more legroom expect to arrive early for it.

Don't lose your bottle!

Tighter airport security can make it harder to transport duty free bottles of alcohol these days. When security is tightest, you might only be allowed to carry unopened 100ml bottles of liquid in your hand luggage (which must be placed in separate, clear bags as you go through security). This presents no problem on direct flights as you only hit duty free after security, but if you have a connecting flight, the only way you will be able to keep your booze is if you can put it into an item of checked luggage. If you can't do this, the security personnel will get an early Christmas present!

Weight limits

Weight limits vary enormously from airline to airline and from route to route, often depending on how much you paid for your ticket. As a guide, long-haul flights tend to allow one item of hand luggage weighing up to 10kg and a maximum of two bags of checked luggage weighing up to 22kg or 25kg each. It's important to check the limits before any flight but especially when security is heightened because allowances can change with little or no warning.

Tipping the scales

While the total weight allowance on some long-haul flights can be as much as 50kg, don't forget that there are still individual limits for each bag (up to 25kg) and if just one is over the limit, you will be charged an excess fee – even if you have not exceeded the total weight allowance. Always check the restrictions before you fly, weigh your bags at home, and pack an empty bag to fill up, just in case.

Budget airlines

One of the ways budget airlines keep their costs down is to restrict luggage allowances. This could be as little as 15kg per person (not per bag) for checked luggage and 5kg for hand luggage, and the charge for exceeding this is significant. This isn't necessarily a bad thing though, as you'll have no choice but to pack lighter bags that are easier to carry.

Beating the weight restriction

If you know you need to transport more than your airline will allow you to carry, the best way around it is to send the heavier, more durable items ahead of you by post. Likewise, if you are away for a long time and find you've bought a lot of souvenirs that you don't want to carry about anymore, look into the cost of sending some home by sea. Just make sure you don't buy or send anything that contravenes customs or export regulations.

Size limits

Again, these vary depending on which airline you fly and the level of security at the time of travel but as a rule of thumb, the dimensions of any checked bag should not exceed 158cm (after you have added the height to the width to the depth), while the dimensions of your hand luggage should not exceed 115cm. In times of heightened security, however, hand luggage allowances could be as little as 96cm, so always check with your airline before you fly.

Hand luggage

Hand luggage falls into two camps. If you like to travel light, it's a good idea not to overfill your hand luggage to keep room for a book or bottle from the Duty Free shops. But if you pack a lot when you travel, your hand luggage is perfect for single items that are either heavy, valuable, or delicate as they are less likely to be lost or damaged in transit.

Duty-free

Duty-free goods in the airport are always cheaper than they are in the shops but they are often more expensive at your departure airport than they are at your destination airport – especially when flying from the U.K. The cheapest place to buy cigarettes is Africa and the Middle East, for electrical goods it's the Far East, while for wine and beer, continental European countries are a good bet. For a definitive guide of where to get the best value see **www.dutyfreeshoppingindex.com**, which compares duty-free prices between airports worldwide.

"I did not fully understand the dread term "terminal illness" until I saw Heathrow for myself.

Dennis Potter

Prohibited items

This doesn't just cover drugs and guns but even innocuous items like nail clippers and cigarette lighters. Even bottles of mineral water can be banned when security is tightest so check with your airline before you fly to see what's in force. Whenever flying to a camping holiday, make sure you can buy the canisters for your gas stove at your destination before packing, because no airline will accept them on the plane. Scuba diving canisters can usually be transported as long as they are depressurised.

Can't have creases?

If you're flying to a wedding or an important business meeting and you don't want to crease your suit or dress, keep it covered on the hanger and carry it onto the plane as an additional item of hand luggage (most airlines will let you carry a small bag as well). When you board, ask the flight attendant if they will hang it on the coat rail in first class. But don't forget to collect it!

Baggage receipts

These are the little barcodes attached to your boarding pass that match the flight labels on your checked bags. Don't lose them! If your bags go missing, you will need the receipts to get them back. If your bags are lost and you're left without clothes for more than a day, ask the airline to pay for replacements.

Dealing with delays

Delays are an inevitable hazard of flying that no one enjoys – especially on short breaks. To make sure it doesn't ruin your holiday, find out your new arrival time and get the airline to check that you can still reach your final destination safely at that time of day. If there's any chance you'll be left stranded, ask your airline to help you make alternative arrangements.

Stranded at the airport

If your flight is heavily delayed or even cancelled, your airline has a responsibility to look after you while you wait. In the U.K., for a two-hour delay they should supply a drink, a snack and two phone calls, for example. If you're delayed overnight, they should arrange dinner and accommodation for you – so make sure you don't pay for it yourself.

Short transfers

If you have a short transfer between international flights, don't panic – the plane shouldn't leave without you. All airports have a specified 'minimum connection time' and if your transfer is below this limit, there should be a contingency that allows you to be fast-tracked through to your connecting flight. If you are in any doubt, check with airline officials during check-in and again before you leave the plane to ensure you can be accommodated. The greatest risk with quick connections is that your bags don't make it onto the same plane.

Top 10
natural travel Wonders of the World

1 Serengeti Animal Migration (Kenya & Tanzania).

2 Galapagos Islands (Pacific Ocean – off Ecuador).

3 Grand Canyon (Southwest USA).

4 Iguazu Falls (Brazil & Argentina).

5 Amazon Rain Forest (Mainly Brazil & Peru).

6 Ngorongoro Volcanic Crater (Tanzania).

7 Great Barrier Reef (Northeast Australia).

8 Victoria Falls (Zambia & Zimbabwe).

9 Bora Bora Island (French Polynesia).

10 Cappadocia Caves & Rocks (Central Turkey).

Airport navigation

Remember, especially with a family, that your holiday begins as soon as you enter the departure hall so be determined to make the whole experience an enjoyable one. This can be a cumbersome task but, with a little preparation, it needn't be. First, if you can, check in online before you leave home and leave plenty of time to get to the airport. Let the kids carry their own backpacks with music, books, toys, or games but keep all the tickets and passports together in a single wallet for safety. As soon as you're through security, find a base and make sure everyone's occupied.

DID YOU KNOW?
Japan's Kitakyushu Airport was built on a man-made island three kilometres off-shore in the Seto Sea.

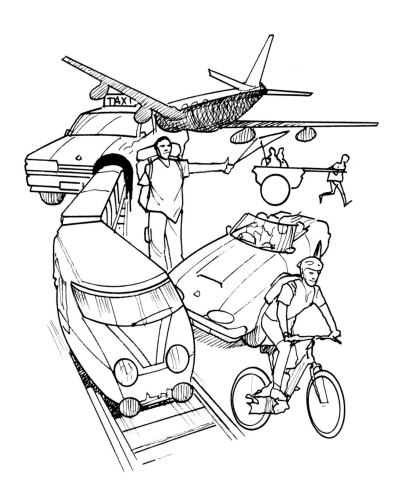

chapter 5
Travelling with ease

Flying

Some people love flying, other people hate it, but we all want it to go smoothly. Here's how. First, wear comfortable clothes that are easy to wash. (How many cartons of orange juice have you burst on an airplane?) Second, eat a good meal at least two hours before you fly and avoid eating too much on the flight itself. The reduced pressure restricts blood flow and makes digestion more difficult. Third, for the same reason, keep moving about to avoid cramps, and reduce the risk of DVT (Deep Vein Thrombosis) by walking around the cabin every hour or so and wiggling your feet regularly. Fourth, keep hydrated by drinking plenty of water and avoid drinking too much fruit juice or alcohol.

Quick tip

PLANE AIR

The cabin of an airplane isn't pressurised to sea level conditions and this is what makes air travel so tiring. The air is drier and of lower quality, too, so it's a good idea to keep well hydrated and boost your immune system with plenty of fresh fruit and vegetables and perhaps the odd vitamin supplement before you fly.

Jetlag

Beating jetlag is all about resetting your body clock. The first step is to set your watch to your destination time as soon as possible to encourage your body to do the same (see **www.timezoneconverter.com**). Avoid alcohol and sleeping pills as both will leave you feeling groggy and your body adjusts better on its own (this is particularly important if you are expecting to drive a hire car from the airport when you arrive). For longer flights, when jet lag is more severe, the earlier you start preparing yourself, the better. A good source of advice can be found at **www.bodyclock.com**, which shows you how to alter your routine in the run up to your flight in order to minimise the impact of the time change when you arrive.

Long-haul

When a flight seems like it's going on forever, get the world map open at the back of the in-flight magazine and break the journey down into sections. Every time you cross one of the boundaries reward yourself with a walk around the cabin or a light snack. Sleep is a great way to pass the time but if you can't drop off, keep yourself occupied with a puzzle or a good book and avoid those free movies. Before you know it, you'll be either snoozing happily or approaching your final descent. For smokers, nicotine replacements will help smooth the journey along.

Contact lenses

If you use contact lenses, don't wear them on a flight as the dry air in the cabin will make them uncomfortable and difficult to remove. The best place to keep them is in your hand luggage though, as the lower pressure in the hold can draw the solution out of the container and dry them to a crisp.

Nodding off

The secret to a good sleep on a journey is to recreate the conditions you normally sleep in at home: in a dark, quiet, comfortable place. This is not always easy but the trick is to use an inflatable neck cushion with ear plugs and eye shades. Be careful if you are carrying valuables though as sensory deprivation makes an easy street for pickpockets.

Quick tip

SLIP ON, SLIP OFF
Another effect of flying is that your feet swell up. If you leave your shoes on, by the time you touchdown your feet can be very uncomfortable. It's a good idea to wear shoes that you can easily slip off and on again. No one likes a wet sock when they visit the toilet.

Best seat on the plane

If you prefer a smooth ride the most stable part of the plane is between the wings. In heavy turbulence the seats towards the back of the plane always lurch higher.

"There are only two emotions in a plane: boredom and terror.

Orson Welles

Road trips

On long road trips the more traffic you encounter, the more tiring the drive will be, so adjust your stops accordingly. Water can be just as good at keeping a driver alert as coffee and it's important to keep well hydrated all the way. If you find drinking difficult while driving, use a bladder-type container with a hose attached (available from most camping stores) as you can safely drink from these hands-free and take smaller sips to cut down on toilet breaks.

Driving overseas

If you're going to be driving a car overseas, make sure you know the rules of the road beforehand as there are always anomalies. In the centre of Melbourne, Australia, for example, if you want to turn right at a cross roads you need to get into the far left hand lane and wait for the light to go green on the road to your immediate left before pulling out in front of the traffic to your right. Sound scary? It is. For a good source of advice, see **www.drivingabroad.co.uk**.

Long distance, own steam

If you are driving long distance in a remote area like the outback of Australia, make sure you have at least two days' supply of water per person, ready made radiator coolant, some dried fruit and nuts, a fully inflated spare tyre, engine oil, a jack, duct tape, a knife, first aid kit, matches, and a spare fan belt. A survival tips book might come in handy too.

No A/C

If you're driving in unbearable heat and have no air conditioning in the car (or not enough petrol in the tank to turn it on) a good way to keep cool is to soak your shirt in water and leave the window down while you let it air dry on you.

Train journeys

Travelling by train is one of the most relaxing, most soporific ways to get around. But if you're travelling alone you don't want to have to keep checking your bags to see if they're still there every time the train stops. The solution is to carry a lock and chain to attach them to the rack, or a custom-made PacSafe mesh (see **www.pac-safe.com**) which will also make them slash proof. You'll sleep a lot easier knowing no one can get into your gear.

Bus journeys

Travelling by bus overseas is a great way to meet people. But security can be a problem so use a money belt for your valuables and keep it tucked beneath your clothes rather than out on show as it's a prime target. You should also keep your valuables on you rather than in the luggage compartment as it's been known for stowaways to board tourist buses and rifle through the bags below while everyone sleeps quietly above.

Best seat on the bus

Always go for the front. You will feel the bumps and corners a lot less and can get off and on a lot easier when it stops. It's also a good idea to work out which side the sun is on during the journey as an afternoon in direct sunlight can wither even the hardiest traveller.

Cycling holidays

Cycling holidays are a fantastic way to see a country and get to know its people, but always check the weather conditions before you go. A bike is no way to travel in a monsoon. Training is also vital as a week in the saddle can really take its toll. For efficient riding, keep a smooth motion by peddling quickly in a high gear rather than peddling slowly in a low gear.

Sailing off into the sunset

As oil prices rise and we become more sensitive to the impact of air travel on the environment, travelling by boat is likely to make a real comeback. From yachts to freighters there are ships to suit every budget and every taste, and there is no better place to realise the old travelling philosophy that happiness is a journey, not a destination.

Quick tip

ALL AT SEA

Where there are boats, there are shaky sea legs. If you're prone to sea-sickness, the best way to avoid it is to stay outside on deck right from the start of the journey and keep your eyes focused on the horizon. This gives your brain a chance to adjust to the unexpected sway of the boat.

Tackling travel sickness

Ginger and peppermint are great natural remedies for travel sickness but if you're already feeling ill, the last thing you want is to be eating roots and leaves. Fresh air is the ticket to calming your stomach but if you can't get any, take long, slow, deep breaths instead as this stimulates a similar, balancing response in the nervous system. You should also keep your head raised and your eyes open.

Top 10
romantic islands of the World

1. French Polynesian Islands.
2. Bali Island.
3. Fiji Islands.
4. Seychelles Islands.
5. Hawaiian Islands.
6. Greek Islands.
7. Madeira Islands.
8. Cook Islands.
9. Caribbean Islands.
10. Bermuda Island.

Taxis

Taxis are notorious booby traps for travellers, with many horror stories of extra zeros added to fares and unwitting travellers being dropped off on the wrong side of town. But they're still a great way to get around and learn about a city. Who knows the place better than a cabbie, after all? First ask a local how much the journey should cost you, then choose a registered, metered cab, agree on your fare before you get in and write it down so the driver can acknowledge it. If they don't, find another cab.

Taxi fares

One of the things you always want to know when you arrive in a new airport is how much the taxi ride to the city will cost. The best way to find out is to ask the person sitting next to you on the plane. It's a fair bet that they've been there before and who knows, you might even get to share the ride.

Rickshaws and tuk-tuks

Cheap and fun to ride, three-wheeled rickshaws and 'tuk-tuks' in Asia were once a traveller's best friend. But be aware that they aren't all that safe on the roads and due to their novelty value they're often more expensive than regular taxis. It's essential to agree on a price before you set off and if the driver offers to show you his friend's shop on the way, politely but firmly decline (unless you want to go and see the shop of course). As a rule, if you need to get somewhere quickly and safely, it's probably best to avoid them.

Quick tip

GO BY FOOT

An underground train or packed bus rarely gives the best view of a city so to see more of the place and get your bearings, go by foot instead. There is no better way to get to know it than from the ground up.

Go against the flow

Tourist attractions can become a bit of a treadmill at times, with people literally falling over each other to see the sights. To avoid the wandering herds, vary your routes from what's suggested in the guidebook (try walking them in reverse, for example) and ask a local if they'd suggest anywhere else you should see. Remember, a guidebook never tells the whole story.

DID YOU KNOW?

The first flight was made in 1783 by the Montgolfier Brothers who, watched by onlooking Marie Antoinette and King Louis XVI of France, took a sheep, duck, and cockerel with them into the sky in a hot air balloon.

chapter 6

chapter 6
Travelling with the family

The perfect family holiday

Always a tall order, but the best family holidays are those that have something for everyone. Think carefully about what every family member would enjoy before you book, and find something that caters for as many tastes as possible. Toddlers and teenagers can be the most difficult to satisfy so adjust your expectations accordingly.

Healthy eating

Good food is essential for a good family holiday. Your choice of destination should offer cuisine that you can all enjoy and be careful to avoid anywhere with questionable hygiene. Bacteria that are harmless to adults can be very dangerous to young children. To make sure everyone stays healthy, take multi-vitamins and hydration salts with you as back-up.

Quick tip

A PHOTOGRAPHIC MEMORY
Always carry photographs of your children on holiday (or email them to a web based account) in case you're ever separated and they become lost. Even if you're faced with an insurmountable language barrier, you can still give a perfect description to the police.

Flying with children

Many long-haul flights have games consoles plugged into the back of the seats but don't always count on them working. Wherever you're flying, pack plenty of games to keep the kids occupied and if they get restless give them a drink and a sweet to suck on. Not as a treat, but to help balance the cabin pressure that will be affecting their ears more than your own.

Ear planes

These are special, travel ear plugs designed to reduce pain during take-off and landing by using special filters to ease the pressure. You can get them from most travel shops and some chemists, but keep a good supply if you travel a lot as they only work for one or two journeys. Smaller sizes are available for children.

Safe journeys

If you are on a long journey with children and want to get some sleep, make sure you sit on the outside in an aisle seat so if they do need to get out, they'll have to wake you first and you'll always know where they are.

Family fees

One of the biggest drawbacks to a family holiday is that you're always travelling in peak season. You can reduce the cost by booking late but your choices may be limited, so whenever you book always ask for child discounts. They can be up to 10% less than the full price and remember, babies often travel free.

Home comforts

If you take young children on holiday it's a good idea to pack their pillowcases as well as a few of their favourite toys. The room will feel a lot more like home once you've got the toys on the bedside table and the pillowcases over the pillows. Make sure they are distinctive though as it's easy to forget them if they are the same colour as the sheets.

Peak season?

Sometimes the only thing peaking in peak season is the year's rainfall. Peak season is determined by the school holiday schedule not the best weather conditions, so make sure you get your money's worth by finding out exactly which season you'll be travelling into before you book. It's never a guarantee of good weather, but at least you're prepared.

Bring education to life

A great way to make lessons more interesting next year at school is to take the family to visit places that are covered on the syllabus. When you've seen sixty-year-old bombs lying unexploded next to the battlefields of the Somme, or walked the mountain paths crossed by Hannibal and his elephants, it brings the lesson to life. If you ever need to take the kids out of school for a holiday (and to avoid peak season prices), this might also persuade the teacher it's a good idea.

Carry on camping

Just the idea of camping can leave some of us in need of a holiday, but don't knock it until you've tried it! Firstly, it's a cheap way to go, and secondly, most campsites are well geared up for families, with pools, playgrounds, and day nurseries ready to take on the kids. The other great thing about camping with the family is the camaraderie you find among other campers that you don't normally get in a hotel.

Kids' club

It's not just campsites that have fun facilities for kids. If, on your next holiday, you're looking for a bit of time off for yourself as well as for the children, let a resort or a cruise ship with a kids' club give you all a break. See websites like **www.childfriendly.co.uk** for advice.

Quick tip

BABY WIPES

Not just for babies! They're an essential item for any trip but especially when you're travelling with the family. When you've been on the road for a long time, wet-wipes are a great way to freshen up. Hand sanitiser is also extremely useful, keeping your hands clean when there's no soap or water to wash them.

"That's the wonderful thing about family travel: it provides you with experiences that will remain locked forever in the scar tissue of your mind.

Dave Barry

Top 10

family holidays

1. Camping on the south coast of France.

2. Keeping fit on a water sports holiday in the Mediterranean.

3. Exploring the ancient temples of Jordan.

4. Enjoying a traditional family Christmas in Finland.

5. Following the 500km Dinosaur Trail in Queensland, Australia.

6. Kayaking through the calm waters of Croatia's Dalmatian coast.

7. Mixing snorkelling with pyramids and camel safaris in Egypt.

8. Finding lost civilisations in the mountains of Peru.

9. Relaxing on the jungle-fringed beaches of Costa Rica.

10. Meeting the elephant orphans of Sri Lanka.

Family bags

Too much luggage can really slow you down on a family holiday – especially with young children. The best bet is to pack as much as you can into your own bags and make sure the youngest don't have to carry much at all. Backpacks with removable day-packs are ideal as you can attach your child's bag to your own when it gets too much for them.

Stop the squabbles

A good way to stop in-fighting on a long journey with children is to have a pick-n-mix bag of toys and treats to hand. Before anything gets too heated, hand the bag around and let the squabblers pick their own amusement.

Holiday scraps

Another way to give the children something to remember their holidays by is to encourage them to collect local memorabilia like ticket stubs, visitor leaflets and postcards that they can compile into a scrapbook. It's a good idea to buy the scrapbook when you arrive, as it will be more unique to the destination.

Creative genius

The relaxation time you get on holiday can be an inspired source of creativity, so why not capture some of it in a sketchbook on your next trip? Family drawings of the places you visit make better souvenirs than photographs.

Go the write way

Travel journals make bestsellers these days, so why not encourage the family to keep their own? Always buy the notebooks overseas as they are fantastic souvenirs and will make fascinating reading years later. Encourage your children to note down all the questions they have about the places they visit – not just the details – as this will inspire their natural curiosity. You never know, you might have another Bill Bryson on your hands.

A ROOM WITH A VIEW

We all want a hotel room with a view, but if you're travelling with children make sure the window can't be easily unlocked so they're not likely to fall out. Similarly if you have a balcony, as soon as you arrive make sure it's safe and fit for family use.

Don't be shocked

Electricity supplies are not always as safe overseas as they are at home so take care whenever using transformer plugs; always check the bathroom for any power points that could come into contact with water, and make sure all the heaters or air conditioning units have been properly safety tested before switching them on.

House swaps

A great way to take the family on holiday without losing all the conveniences of home is to arrange a house swap with a family from another country. It's cost effective and gets you away from the tourist traps. The cheapest way is to make your own arrangements with friends overseas, but agencies like **www.homelink.org.uk** and **www.homebase-hols.com** can also arrange things for you.

chapter 7
Making the most of your holiday

Take a gift

If you live in Kendal, take mint cake. If you're from Kentucky, take bourbon! Something unique to your home – however ordinary it seems when you're there – takes on a completely different value overseas and will make a very special gift for someone you meet. In northern India, for example, Levi's jeans are highly valued.

Don't forget your roots

Take photos of your friends and family and even postcards of your home town with you on holiday. You might want to get away from it all, but the people you meet will be fascinated to see where you've come from, and the shared understanding will create an instant bond between you.

Writing home

Ever promised everyone a postcard and sent none? Give yourself a head start by printing address labels from your computer before you leave and then attach them to a set of postcards as soon as you arrive. You've got the whole holiday to write the messages and no excuse for not sending them!

Hand washing

Washing your clothes by hand is not something we have to do very often these days, but it's very useful if you can do it well while travelling. The trick is good old fashioned elbow grease. It's no good leaving dirty clothes out in a bowl to sunbathe! You've got to get in there and give them a proper kneading. Take travel wash with you as some local brands contain bleach that's unsuitable for many fabrics.

Know the customs

It's important you enjoy yourself on holiday, but not at the expense of the local way of life. What is permissible at home might not be overseas – like drinking in public or walking around without a shirt on – and it is your responsibility to be aware of local customs, not the other way round. Read a good country guide before you go to make sure you travel with respect.

Speak the language

The spread of the English language has made us much lazier travellers than we should be, but a little effort to speak the local language goes a very long way. One of the great joys of travelling is the opportunity to learn about another culture but by speaking English everywhere you can miss out.

The right souvenirs

Be careful about the souvenirs you buy. What appears to be in abundant supply in the market could be an endangered species, a protected artefact, or even a substance that is banned back home, all of which will land you in hot water in Customs.

Sign language

Much less satisfying than learning to speak the lingo but
if you find it hard to pick up a new language, draw pictures
to help you communicate instead. If you're not good at drawing,
either, no worries! Use an image search engine like Google
Images to print them off before you go.

Quick tip

TAKE IT EASY...

In a hot climate, have you ever noticed the locals walking
a lot slower than all the tourists? Or been surprised when
you've arrived in a restaurant pouring with sweat when
everyone else is bone dry? That's because you've been
rushing around at the same pace you would back home!
The hotter it is, the slower you need to go.

... Once more, take it easy!

Holidays are all about relaxing, but when things don't happen
as quickly as you might expect, or don't run exactly to plan,
don't sweat about it. The different pace of life is all part of the
joy of travelling and you won't beat them, so just join them.

Go local

If you travel thousands of miles to do all the same stuff you do
at home, it's not really a holiday, is it? The best trips are when
you go local, get into the way of life and broaden your horizons.
That way you're guaranteed a holiday to remember.

I can't think of anything that excites a greater sense of childlike wonder than to be in a country where you are ignorant of almost eveything.

Bill Bryson

Scuba diving

Learning to scuba dive is something many people get into when they are in a far off exotic location. A globally recognised qualification is PADI (**www.padi.com**) and from their website you can find all the accredited dive centres worldwide. The cost of getting a certificate varies a lot but one of the cheapest places to learn is Central America. Only expert divers should think about buying and travelling with their own equipment though as it is expensive, heavy, difficult to transport, and dive schools always supply it anyway.

Trekking

The beauty of trekking when you travel is that you can get into remote and awe-inspiring environments completely under your own steam. Hotspots like New Zealand, Chile, Morocco, and Nepal often supply guides (and on some routes they are mandatory) but with experience and a good map, it is possible to go on your own. Lightweight gear, a good sleeping bag, and water purification equipment are all essential, as are a well broken-in pair of shoes. Before you leave home, it's also worth finding out what accommodation and cuisine is available so you know whether to pack a tent (shelters are often available on popular routes) and your own stove and food. If in doubt, always bring supplies of the latter as specialised, pre-prepared food packs are hard to get overseas.

Volunteer work

Volunteering overseas is hard work but it's the best way to get to know another culture. It doesn't sound like much of a holiday but it could be the most refreshing, most enlightening break you ever take. Travel has a massive impact on culture and the environment, and as we move towards a more sustainable future it's going to become even more important that we give something back to the places we visit. See **www.responsibletravel.com**, **www.earthwatch.org** or **www.i-to-i.com**.

Leave no trace

Easier said than done, but leaving things the way you found them is not only respectful but increasingly vital as man's environmental impact takes hold. There's a question as to whether air travel can ever be truly sustainable, but a good start would be to make your flight 'carbon neutral' by paying an organisation like **www.climatecare.org** to offset the emissions spent getting to your destination by planting trees and funding sustainable energy projects. Even better, avoid flying altogether on your next holiday.

Quick tip

TAKING PHOTOS RESPECTFULLY
The photos you take of the people you meet abroad are always a treasure. But bear in mind that some cultures view photography very differently from us and you should always ask permission before snapping.

Top 10

adrenaline-rush holidays

1 Heli-skiing in the Himalayas.

2 Venturing into the cloud forests of Ecuador.

3 Horse trekking in the American North West.

4 Driving a 4 x 4 through the Kimberleys in Western Australia.

5 Grizzly bear spotting in Alaska.

6 White water rafting in Zambia.

7 Hill walking on the south island of New Zealand.

8 River canoeing in the Canadian wilderness.

9 Venturing into the jungles of Borneo to see the Orangutans.

10 Riding a camel across the Kalahari Desert.

chapter 8
Taking better photographs

Lights, camera, action

A holiday is one long photo-opportunity, so it's worth making the most of it. First, think about light. Light is the essence of a good photo and even the most mundane of subjects can shine in the right conditions. Remember that if your subject is between you and the sun, you won't pick out much detail, so keep the sun either behind you or to one side.

Dawn and dusk

The start and end of the day are golden times for the travel photographer. You'll find the most dramatic lighting with softer glows adds depth to colour, and character to the darker areas. If you take a photo in the middle of the day, think about where the sun will cast the heaviest shadow.

Quick tip

GOOD COMPOSITION
A good trick to improve all your photos is to compose them in thirds rather than placing your subject right in the middle. This gives the finished product more balance and allows the background to become as interesting as the subject.

People shots

Despite the moans of the family, it's always a good idea to include people in your photos. Endless landscapes, however beautiful, can lose their appeal over time. With people in the foreground even a bad photo will tell you something about the experiences you shared. A good trick is to try to include their whole body in the photo, rather than cutting them off at the knee or waist, which can make the photo look amateurish.

One in the eye

Whenever you take photos of people or animals, always try to take them at their eye level. This is easy when your subject is the same height as you, but more difficult when you're taking photos of young children and especially animals. The results will be worth the effort though.

Level headed

It's easy to focus your attention on your subject and forget about what's behind them, but this often leads to a wonky horizon that can ruin the overall shot (especially when you're on a boat). To keep a level head on all your photos, make sure your horizon lines run parallel to the top and bottom of the frame.

Mini tripod

A mini tripod is a handy addition to the travel photographer's kit. With adjustable legs, you can get a level shot no matter how uneven the surface, and get more from your night time photos when longer shutter speeds demand a rock steady lens. Gorillapods are very versatile, available from **www.amazon.com**.

Go digital

With high quality lenses, no film to carry and huge memory storage, digital cameras are ideal for travelling. They take great photos and the display screens make composition easier, while the review and delete options mean you only end up with the best photos. As well as saving space, the memory cards also mean you don't have to worry about sending exposed film through the x-ray at the airport. Just make sure you have plenty of spare batteries as they run out fast.

Web storage

The best place to keep your holiday photos is an online storage facility like **www.snapfish.com** or **www.kodak.com**. They are free, you can upload as many photos as you want, and email a link to your friends while you're still away so they can see what you're up to. When you want to order the prints, just choose the ones you want and they'll post them to your door.

Quick tip

ACTION SHOTS

The autofocus can slow a digital camera down just enough to miss an action shot so this is the time to go manual. You will have to anticipate the shot by having your camera switched on and preset to the right focal point, and then take the photo just before the event so the shutter opens at exactly the right moment.

12 months … 12 festivals

January   Northern Lights Festival, Tromso, Norway. Celebrate the rising of the sun after weeks of winter darkness.

February   Historic Car Rally, Monte Carlo, Monaco. Where better to enjoy the glamorous old days of motoring?

March   Water Drawing Festival, Nara, Japan. A sacred and solemn rite that marks the advent of spring.

April   Bull Running, Gaucín, Spain. Forget the eggs, this Easter celebration involves bulls running in the streets!

May   Marriage of Trees Festival, Accettura, Italy. An ancient fertility ceremony that joins a 'King' and 'Queen' tree in union.

June   Red Earth Festival, Oklahoma City, USA. America's largest celebration of its indigenous culture.

July   Rainforest World Music Festival, Sarawak, Borneo. A tropical Glastonbury, with less mud.

August   Brodick Highland Games, Arran, Scotland. Highland games played out on the stunning Isle of Arran.

September   Henley-on-Todd Regatta, Alice Springs, Australia. A madcap boat race on a dry river bed.

October   Bardolino Wine Festival, Lake Garda, Italy. Fine wine, fantastic food, phenomenal views.

November   Day of the Dead, Todos Santos, Guatemala. A spectacular memorial to lost relatives with horse racing and traditional marimba music.

December   New Year's Eve, Wainui Beach, New Zealand. Be one of the first people to see the New Year dawn.

Recharging your batteries

Despite the advantages, some photographers will tell you to avoid taking a digital camera on holiday as the batteries will run out long before your memory card and recharging them is a problem. It's more difficult than replacing an old lithium battery, but not insurmountable. Using a plug adapter is one option, but if your charger isn't made for the local voltage it can be unreliable. You could buy a new charger when you arrive – but they can be expensive and won't be any use back home. The solution is to take a car charging unit as the 12-volt adapter will work on almost any car cigarette lighter in the world.

Camera safety

Your camera is probably the most delicate item you take on holiday so make sure you get a decent case and sufficient insurance. Soft, durable bags are easier to carry but for complete safety go for a rigid, waterproof container.

Photographic boomerang

To give your camera the best chance of finding its way back to you, start your pictures with a photograph of your name, email address, and mobile phone number with a note saying: 'please contact me if you find this camera!'

Selling your photos

Travel companies and travel magazines are always on the lookout for photos of stunning locations so don't be afraid to put your photos to work to help pay for your next holiday. If they're well composed, focused, and show something unique about the place you visited, they could become much more than holiday snaps. To find out whom to offer them to, go to your local newsagent and copy the phone number and editor's name from the front of the travel magazines and give them a call.

DID YOU KNOW?

Photographs of deceased, indigenous Australians should not be shown for several years after their death out of respect.

"The traveller
sees what he sees.
The tourist sees
what he has
come to see.

G.K. Chesterton

chapter 9
Looking after your money

Money makes the world go round

They say money makes the world go round and that's definitely true where holidays are concerned. If available, you should always change some currency before you go so you can familiarise yourself with the different denominations and be ready to use it as soon as you arrive.

Taking money abroad

The trick is to keep all the bases covered. Traveller's cheques are secure but to avoid heavy exchange charges you'll need large denominations, which can leave you with more cash than you'd like to carry around. ATMs have become a more viable alternative with reliable exchange rates, but the unpredictable fees can still give you a shock on the bank statement. In Britain, some banks don't charge for overseas transactions and if you do a lot of travelling, it's worth shopping around for the right account before you go. Finally, always take a credit or debit card abroad and make sure it is a well known brand like Visa or MasterCard.

Make a crib sheet

Print out an exchange rate crib sheet before you go abroad
so you know at a glance how much you are paying. Make
one column for your own currency and another for the local
currency, and then list ten or twenty equivalent denominations
side by side. Websites like **www.xe.com** or **www.x-rates.com**
can give you the going rates

Withdrawals

If you need to draw money on your bank account overseas
remember that, as well as your bank, most ATMs will also charge
you. To avoid paying twice use your card in a supermarket
and ask for 'cash back' if the service is available. That way
you should only pay for your money at the going exchange rate.

Safe exchange

Backstreet exchange booths may offer lower rates, but the
difference is usually so minimal you have to change a lot
of cash to make any real difference – which is not a risk you
want to take down any backstreet! Stick to legitimate money
changers in well lit, well policed areas.

Ready money

Many countries use U.S. Dollars as secondary or even primary
currency so before you fly find out if it's worth taking some.
Unlike some local currencies, U.S. Dollars won't lose their value
and can be especially useful in an emergency (in Vietnam, for
example, a two dollar bill is worth several times its face value).
Take a range of denominations right down to one dollar bills.

Small is beautiful

Small notes are always more useful, especially in developing countries where large denominations draw attention and can be hard to change. You should also avoid pulling out large wads of cash in public by planning ahead and preparing a stash of smaller notes for the day before you leave the hotel.

Bartering

Bartering is nothing to be ashamed of. In many countries it's a natural and respected part of buying and selling. But at the same time, remember that it's not a sport and shouldn't be done for its own sake. Before starting your negotiations, think how much you'd be willing to pay. If the price is lower than the figure in your head, you've already got a bargain. If the price is higher than you expected, as a rule of thumb, offer 50% and settle at around 75% of the total. Whenever buying expensive items do your research so you know the market rate.

Quick tip

TIPPING

Tips are always hard to quantify so find out what the local custom is before you arrive and be ready to reward good service. More often than not, you'll end up getting better service as a result. A good source of advice can be found at **www.tipping.org**.

Top 10

places to see wild swarms

1 One hundred million red crabs – Christmas Island, Indian Ocean, Australia.

2 Two million wildebeest – Plains of Botswana, North Namibia, South Zimbabwe.

3 Two million jellyfish – Island of Palau.

4 Eighty thousand migrating storks – Ban Thasadet, Thailand.

5 Two million free-tailed bats – the caves of Gunung Mulu National Park, Borneo.

6 Thousands of caribou – Ivvavik National Park, Canadian Arctic.

7 Thousands of squeaking grunions – beaches of southwestern California.

8 Millions of mayflies – Mississippi River, La Crosse, Wisconsin, US.

9 Millions of monarch butterflies – Angangueo, Mexico.)

10 Thousands of turtles – Tamar Project, beaches of the Brazilian coastline.

No money?

If you are overseas and you've been robbed of all your cash, the first place to go is your local embassy which should be able to arrange emergency funds, for a fee payable later. Another option is to speak to a company like Western Union or Money Gram who specialise in wiring money around the world.

Change on the street

If someone asks you to change a large note on the street, politely decline. This is a classic lead into a wallet snatch. Similarly, don't carry all your cash in one pocket and ideally, try to carry a second wallet with a few small notes in it that you are happy to hand over to a mugger without a second thought.

DID YOU KNOW?

The islands of Yap in Micronesia have streets that are literally lined with money. For day-to-day transactions they use U.S. Dollars but the indigenous currency is still highly valued – cut from a limestone quarry and fashioned into circular, stone coins. Some of the coins are so large that they can't be moved and are left to adorn the pathways of local villages.

chapter 10
Travelling on a budget

Book online

There are many good deals available online but look out
for hidden extras. Tax isn't always included in the first price
you're quoted and there might be restrictions on when
and where you can travel. A quick way to compare prices
is to use a 'metacrawler' like **www.airline-network.com**,
www.expedia.com or **www.opodo.com**. But bear in mind
that both prices and availability can change from day-to-day,
from site-to-site. A flight that's fully booked one day, for
example, can be available the next when a new carrier starts
taking bookings.

Don't just fly mid-week, buy mid-week!

It's always cheaper to fly Wednesday-to-Wednesday than
it is to fly Saturday-to-Saturday, but did you know it can also
be cheaper to book your tickets midweek than at the weekend?
It's all down to supply and demand and it stands to reason
that travel companies are likely to set their prices higher when
more people are making their bookings. For the same reason
you should book your summer holidays at the end of the
previous summer and your winter holidays at the end of
the previous winter.

"The alternative to a vacation is to stay home and tip every third person you see.

Anon

Leave it to chance

One of the best ways to get a cheap holiday is to leave your destination to chance and book the best-priced holiday a few days before you go. Weekend travel sections in the newspapers, and websites like **www.lastminute.com** can be good for deals and, in Britain, the TV Teletext service is still worth a look.

Free camping

Camping is one of the cheapest holidays going and did you know that in Britain it's even cheaper to pitch a tent in Scotland than it is in England and Wales? That's because north of the border you can camp 'wild' on public land away from roads and dwellings without having to pay any fees, while further south you are restricted to designated campsites. You won't have the luxury of camp facilities of course, but the pristine views more than make up for it. The golden rule, as ever, is to leave everything as you found it and take everything you brought with you back home again.

Sail away

If time is no object and you're feeling adventurous, one of the most cost-effective ways to see the world is to take a job on a ship: either by crewing a yacht or working on a cruise ship. It's hard work all the way, no doubt, but worth the effort when you arrive in your sun blessed destination with money to burn.

Get bumped

Many flights are overbooked by airlines on the expectation that a few passengers won't show up on the day. But every now and again everyone does show up on the day and there aren't enough seats. So if you're a budget conscious traveller and this happens on your flight, offer to get bumped onto the next as the airline will pay you for the inconvenience. The flipside of this is that if you do want to fly and you don't have a seat, this is your best chance to get a free upgrade to first class!

Student cards

If you're a student and you have a valid student card, always take it on holiday as many countries, particularly in Europe, give student discounts on numerous top tourist attractions. As a back up, you should also take an ISIC card (International Student Identification Card) which you can get from STA Travel (**www.isiccard.com**) and BUNAC (**www.bunac.org**). See **www.isic.org** for more information.

Quick tip

TRAVEL FURTHER

Sometimes what you save on a cheap flight you spend as soon as you leave the airport, so to make sure your holiday stays on budget think about the cost of living in your destination before you book. You might spend more on the airfare but if you can live like royalty on a shoestring budget, it makes a lot of sense.

Work abroad

Some holidays will actually pay you for being there. The best known is TEFL (Teaching English as a Foreign Language) – which is particularly lucrative in the Middle East and Japan – but there are all kinds of ways to work your way around the world. You can arrange packages on the east coast of Australia, for example, where they teach you to sail before giving you a job as a sailing instructor. Speak to your local college or university about where to find a good TEFL course, and for jobs use **www.tefl.com**.

Call in all favours

If you have friends overseas and you want to save a bit of cash, arrange a holiday to go and visit them. Your wallet will be a lot happier and with a local to show you around, you'll get to see a lot more of the place than if you booked into a hotel.

Cook it yourself

Self-catered accommodation can be expensive up front, but once the costs are divided between everyone staying there and you factor in the savings made by not eating out for breakfast, lunch and dinner, you soon save a few bucks.

Cheaper transport

Another bill that mounts up fast on holiday is the cost of transport, especially if you have to get a taxi back to the hotel every night. There are three very simple ways round this: first, make sure your hotel is in walking distance from the major sights, if it's not, hire a bike, and finally use public transport as much as possible. That way you'll save money and meet more people at the same time.

Good training

Many countries offer discounts on long distance train journeys if you book in advance but hammer you on the ticket price if you buy it on the day of travel. In Europe, the best option is a Eurailpass; but wherever you are, always book direct with the train company to get the cheapest ticket and avoid commission.

Get junk mail

It's time to stop hating junk mail because where holidays are concerned, it can save you a packet. First, set up a separate email address so your real address isn't affected, then sign up for as many different travel e-newsletters as possible. Your inbox fills up faster than a pint glass at Oktoberfest, but this is how tour operators shift their underbooked trips so you'll be the first to know about the bargains.

Buy local

If you don't mind leaving things open to chance, try booking your holiday activities when you arrive rather than in advance. That way you'll save on booking fees knowing you're also supporting the local economy, which in many destinations relies on tourist income.

Take a stove

Food always makes a dent in the travel budget so why not take a camping stove with you and cook your own? As long as you've got good weather, it's ideal. What could be better than a steaming hot bowl of pasta with glass of wine on the beach as you watch the sun setting over the waves?

Quick tip

TRAVEL BY NIGHT
Accommodation is usually the single biggest cost on holiday, but if you travel at night you can sleep on the way. It's not a good idea for families, single or business travellers, but if you're with a group of friends it's fine.

Take a sandwich course

Not so you can get a job in Subway but, if you're a student, a year to live and work abroad while studying. It's a fantastic way to discover another culture, learn a new language, and get great work experience at the same time.

Travel for a good cause

Another way to travel on the cheap is to give your time to a good cause when you get there. As well as helping people you'll be driving your cost-of-living way down. You could even fundraise for the trip beforehand to help with the cost and provide supplies for the project. To find a project, research the issues that are affecting the country and approach a local NGO (Non-Government Organisation) to see if they need help, or arrange it through a work placement organisation like VSO (**www.vso.org.uk**) or Peace Corps (**www.peacecorps.gov**).

Use a sleeping sheet

If you're on a tight budget you might not be staying in the most luxurious of hotels, so it's a good idea to take a sleeping sheet with you. This could either be a bed sheet stitched together down one side, a duvet cover or custom-made sleeping bag liner. They can make even the most inhospitable bed feel more like home.

DID YOU KNOW?
The Nazca Lines are 275-metre-long drawings of animals and geometric forms etched into the Peruvian desert which lay undiscovered for 1,500 years until the first plane flew over the area in 1927.

Top 10
largest islands in the World

		Sq. Mi	Sq. km
1	Greenland	839,999	2,175,597
2	New Guinea	309,000	800,310
3	Borneo	287,300	744,107
4	Madagascar	227,000	587,930
5	Baffin Island, Canada	195,926	507,448
6	Sumatra, Indonesia	182,859	473,605
7	Honshu, Japan	89,176	230,966
8	Great Britain	88,795	229,979
9	Victoria Island, Canada	83,896	217,291
10	Ellesmere, Canada	73,057	189,218

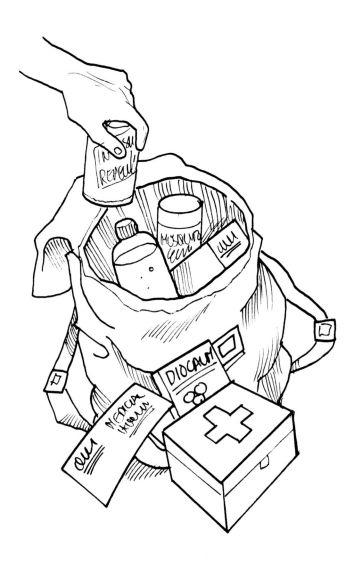

chapter 11
Keeping healthy

Medical notes

Even if you are in perfect health you should always carry medical notes overseas with details of your blood type, any medication you're taking and any significant medical conditions you've had, preferably translated into the local language. If you need treatment it could save your life.

Emergency contacts

Another essential item to keep in a safe place is a list of emergency contacts. They should include contact details of your home doctor, your hotel address, your local Embassy, your next-of-kin, and your airline or tour operator. If you get into trouble at least you, or someone else, will know who to call.

Free health insurance

In Europe many countries have reciprocal health agreements that allow travelling citizens to use their hospitals free of charge. British citizens can take advantage of this by completing an E111 form at the Post Office, but you should always have travel insurance as well. For those living outside Britain, contact your local health department or health insurer to see what you're covered for.

Travel insurance

Wherever you travel, don't leave home without good insurance. You should be insured for the loss of belongings, health care, legal bills, personal liability and, with security issues ever present, curtailment and cancellation. Always read the small print and remember that the best policies are rarely the cheapest. Websites like **www.moneysupermarket.com** or **www.confused.com** can help you compare what's on offer.

Quick tip

WILD AT HEART
If you're planning on taking a raft down a white water ravine or plunging off a bridge with only a rubber cord to save you from certain death, make sure your travel insurance covers you for it. Many policies include extreme sports but note that skiing and professional sports require special cover.

In an emergency

When you are a long way from home, you want to be sure that your insurance company can get you out of trouble – especially in a developing country – so ask what international assistance and emergency repatriation cover they provide. Don't just assume it's included. Find out which organisation they will liaise with (like **www.internationalsos.com**, for example) and whether this organisation operates where you're going to be.

Best laid plans

If you're booking with a tour operator, one of the things you're paying for is their responsibility to get you out of trouble if something goes wrong. Test how well prepared they are by asking what procedures they have in place to deal with an overseas emergency like a terrorist threat or natural disaster. If they are diligent, they will employ consultants like Docleaf (**www.docleaf.com**) to advise them and provide detailed contingency plans.

Simple steps to better health

One of the easiest ways to become ill anywhere is to not wash your hands properly or frequently enough. This can be especially difficult on holiday when you are relying on public conveniences and you are running on someone else's schedule (on a tour, for example). So to bridge the gap between washbasins always take alcohol based hand sanitiser with you.

Safer jabs

If you're travelling to a country where resources are scarce – particularly the developing countries of Asia, South America and Africa – always take your own syringes and needles in case you're hospitalised and need an injection. This preserves local equipment and gives you the reassurance that yours is sterile. Always pack them in your checked luggage though.

Medical kit

You should take a first aid kit on every trip, even if you're just heading off in the car for a weekend away. It should contain the following:

- pain killers
- tweezers
- stomach medicine
- anti-inflammatory tablets
- anti-histamine tablets
- pain killers
- antiseptic lotion
- aftersun
- water purification tablets
- plasters
- blister patches
- bandages
- a thermometer
- matches (in a waterproof case)
- condoms
- prescription medication (if you are taking it) to last as long as you're away

Vaccinations and inoculations

Before you travel, be sure to check whether you require vaccinations, inoculations or preventative medication for diseases like Hepatitis, Yellow Fever or Malaria. In Britain, most are available free through the NHS but some, like the jabs for Rabies and Japanese Encephalitis, might only be available privately. To get an idea of what you need see **www.traveldoctor.co.uk**, but always remember to consult your doctor. Plan well ahead as some courses take several weeks to take effect.

Malaria

People say the best way to avoid Malaria is to not get bitten in the first place, but even for the most diligent repellent-sprayers, that's pretty unrealistic. If you're travelling to an area where the disease is prevalent, be sure to take the correct medication (see your doctor for advice) and don't believe for a minute the old yarn about the tablets simply masking the disease; anti-malarials effectively inhibit its development and the last thing you want is full blown malaria.

Mosquitoes

The active ingredient in most mosquito repellents is a chemical called 'diethyl-m-toluamide' or DEET for short. If you are travelling in the tropics, or any area where there are disease-carrying mosquitoes, use a repellent with at least 50% DEET concentration. However, don't rely on DEET alone as it's not 100% effective and can be harmful when used over prolonged periods (especially to children). Keep covered as much as possible and avoid being outside at dawn and dusk when the bugs are most active.

Natural alternatives

The best natural mosquito repellent is citronella oil. Less harmful and often cheaper than DEET, it is ideal for longer trips when you'll be living with the mossies night after night. To stop you dreaming of helicopters buzzing in your ears, take a fine mesh mosquito net that's been treated in repellent to hang over your bed.

> If you reject
> the food, ignore
> the customs, fear
> the religion and
> avoid the people,
> you might better
> stay home.

James Michener

Top 10
highest mountains in the World

		Feet	Metres
1	Everest, Nepal / Tibet	29,035	8,850
2	K2, Pakistan / China	28,250	8,611
3	Kanchenjunga, India / Nepal	28,169	8,586
4	Lhotse I, Nepal / Tibet	27,940	8,516
5	Makalu I, Nepal / Tibet	27,766	8,463
6	Cho Oyu, Nepal / Tibet	26,906	8,201
7	Dhaulagiri, Nepal	26,795	8,167
8	Manaslu I, Nepal	26,781	8,163
9	Nanga Parbat, Pakistan	26,660	8,125
10	Annapurna, Nepal	26,545	8,091

Zap don't scratch

If mosquito bites send you scratch crazy you've got three solutions. The first is to take an anti-histamine tablet, but these often make you drowsy so they're not always practical. Another option is to use aloe vera gel to naturally soothe the skin. By far the most effective solution, however, is a special mosquito bite 'zapper' which sends a tiny, perfectly safe, electrical pulse through the bite to satisfy the itch, stop you from scratching, and prevent scarring. Available from **www.nomadtravel.co.uk**.

Sun stroke

There's something even worse than getting sand in your swimming trunks on the beach, and that's getting sun stroke. To avoid it, stay hydrated, keep your skin covered and keep out of direct sunlight. If you develop a headache, nausea, dizziness, high fever and small pupils, get help and call a doctor immediately. Emergency treatment can be administered by getting into a cold bath and pressing a cold towel into the back of your neck.

After sun

Not something you want to get caught without on a sunny holiday. There are many types of after sun and the best contain both aloe vera and mosquito repellent. When sun burn is at its worst, there's nothing quite as soothing as aloe vera; and nothing quite as painful as putting on stingy mosquito repellent afterwards!

Over enjoying

No matter where you travel, there's usually a morning after a night of drinking too much. Curing a hangover is all about getting rehydrated, but in a hot climate it can be hard to take in enough water to make up the deficit. To get the salts you need to sort you out, supplement your water intake with a rehydration sachet.

Diarrhoea

The most common of all travel ailments. Antimotility medication like Imodium is essential for journeys and will stop you from losing too much water. The body will often recover quickly on its own so the most important thing you can take is water and rehydration salts. A very effective stomach medicine is Pepto-Bismol which treats indigestion, nausea and diarrhoea, and kills bacteria. If your symptoms don't clear up in 72 hours or you have a fever, see a doctor.

Make mine an H$_2$O

Most of us don't drink enough water when we're at home, but when we travel to a hotter climate than we are used to, it's even harder to drink as much as we need. In the tropics, you might need as many as 15 litres a day. Be careful though as too much water can be as dangerous as too little.

Altitude sickness

Altitude sickness generally occurs above altitudes of 3,000 metres but everyone has a different level of tolerance. Symptoms include headache, dizziness and nausea leading to vomiting, insomnia and in extreme cases, cerebral or pulmonary oedema. The only really effective treatment is to descend. Before travelling to a mountainous region, find out how high the destination airport is, as some − like La Paz in Bolivia − are high enough to induce altitude sickness the moment you touch down.

DVT

Deep Vein Thrombosis hit the headlines as 'economy class syndrome' but it can happen in any type, and class, of journey − not just on airplanes. A blood clot forms within a vein, usually deep within the leg, which is rare but potentially fatal. Taking regular walks, avoiding sleeping for too long when sitting upright, taking aspirin, keeping well hydrated and keeping the blood moving by raising your heels and wiggling your toes regularly will all help avoid it.

chapter 12
Staying safe

Tamper-proof bags

You can be separated from your bags for a long time when you travel so it's a good idea to make sure they are locked and secure. At best, if the security staff need to search your bag they will simply break open the lock and leave you a sticker to let you know. At worst, if someone has tampered with your bag and planted something in it (this has happened), you'll know as soon as you collect it and can alert the police before it goes any further. A cheap way to seal your bag is to wrap it in cling film, and some airports now offer this service in departure halls.

Culture shock

Ever felt totally bewildered in the first few hours of arriving in a new country? That's culture shock. It's a natural reaction, but it can also leave you disoriented and vulnerable to people who don't have your best interests at heart. To beat it, have a plan of attack when you first arrive, know your destination and pre-book your onward travel plans to give you somewhere to head to. It may cost you a bit more up front, but the security and peace of mind are well worth it.

X-ray vision

Most airport security scanners are safe for both camera film and laptops but it's always worth checking with the personnel standing by them if you're in any doubt. Something to watch with these items, though, is the conveyor belt at the other end because even under airport CCTV cameras, it can be a hunting ground for thieves.

Don't forget the padlocks

It's a good idea to use a bag with zips that are designed to be locked with padlocks for security. Combination locks give you fewer keys to lose, but if you use more than one don't set them all to the same code as this makes it twice as easy for someone to figure it out. Of course this means it's twice as hard to remember them as well, but if memory is a problem, email the codes to a web-based email account.

Secure baggage labels

If your bags go missing in transit you don't want someone to get your name and address from the label and know you're not at home. A safer alternative is to use a service like **www.bagsreunited.com** or **www.yellowtag.com** that will register your details on their database and issue you with a unique label that means your bags can be returned to you without your personal details being compromised.

Remove the old labels

If you do a lot of travelling and you still have the old baggage labels attached from your previous flight, make sure you remove them before checking your bags onto your next flight. Otherwise they could be doing a lot more travelling than you!

Jewellery

Leave all the good stuff at home. Wearing expensive jewellery when you travel makes you a magnet to thieves who know immediately that you have more money than most. Furthermore, travel insurance rarely covers single, expensive items.

Wedding rings for single women

One item of jewellery that single women might want to take with them on holiday is a fake wedding ring (unless you are looking for a man, of course). They can be a good defence against the amorous advances of unwanted suitors.

Don't give them a chance

It's easy to become a target on holiday so don't make it easy for pickpockets by leaving your valuables on show. Small rucksacks are easy to unzip as you walk along unaware, so if you do leave a camera or something valuable in there, make sure the bag is secure. Specially designed, lockable zips are advisable.

TIE A YELLOW RIBBON
A brightly coloured ribbon tied around your bags will make them much easier to spot on the baggage reclaim – especially if your suitcase is square and black like all the rest.

Hide your security wallet

Security wallets, or money belts, are useful as long as they are kept out of sight in public at all times. If yours is on show it's immediately obvious that you're carrying all your cash on you and it's all too easy for someone to cut the straps and walk away. If you need to get money from it, do it discreetly where you can't be seen.

Make it a chest strap

When you travel, you should wear any single-strap bag across your chest. If you leave it loosely slung over one shoulder it's easy to swipe. You should also make sure the strap is sturdy enough to resist a knife slash.

Take your room key

It's not a good idea to leave your room keys behind reception in a hotel as it advertises that you're not there to look after your stuff. The same goes for 'Please Clean My Room' signs – it's much better to use 'Please Do Not Disturb' and clean it yourself.

Keep an eye on your passport

Even more than your airfare, your passport is your ticket home. Losing your passport overseas is a headache to be avoided at all costs. Whenever hiring a car, for example, always try to leave something else as a deposit because your passport could be worth more on the black market than the car itself. In hotels it can be hard to avoid leaving your passport but if you can leave a driving licence instead, do.

Check it out before you check in

When you arrive in a hotel, always ask to see the room before you check in. They are less likely to palm you off with a bad room and if they refuse, you know to go somewhere else straight away. Unless a disability prevents you from doing so, it's also safer to get a room on the first or second floor rather than the ground.

Quick tip

WEDGE IT

A good way to sleep safe and sound is to take a door wedge with you and place it beneath the door at night time. Even if someone gets past the lock, you know they're not getting any further without waking you up.

Taxi scam

To avoid losing everything when a taxi driver drives away, never pay for your fare until you have collected all your belongings from the cab.

Hire car scam

It's been known for car jackers to deliberately drive into hire cars and, as soon as the bewildered tourist gets out to inspect the damage, to jump in and drive off with all their belongings. If you're ever involved in an accident in a hire car overseas, stay put, get the other person's details, and go straight to the police.

Buy now, pay later

Whenever paying for goods or services up front always get a receipt. If it's a service you're paying for, it's essential you get all the inclusions written down and signed by whoever is providing them. That way you won't be short changed or landed with an unexpected price hike. Be especially careful when booking tours that go across borders as it's easy for unscrupulous operators not to honour the full deal.

Getting the right directions

Try to get directions from public officials as they are less likely to send you the wrong way. If there are none around, ask more than one person for the same directions, just to be sure.

Finding your way around

Remember that locally bought maps are not always accurate – particularly in remote areas. The best are sometimes only available from specialist map stores back home, so plan ahead. Also be wary of any map that marks out a disputed territory because it can be a criminal offence to carry one in a country that is staking a claim over that territory. Back in the city, another good tip is to avoid pulling out a town map in confusion on a street corner as it can make you a target for thieves. Instead, study your map back at the hotel and figure out the key local landmarks that will show you how to get back to your hotel. The skyline always gives the best pointers so look up as soon as you leave the hotel.

Quick tip

SHORTCUTS
Avoid them at all costs. When you don't know a city, what looks like a good shortcut can quickly leave you lost in a dodgy part of town. Stick to the main routes.

Face-on

Whenever walking on the roads, face into the traffic so you can see what's coming and you're not at risk of cars pulling up behind you. It's also a bad idea to stereotype pickpockets. They can be young or old, male or female and it always happens when you least expect it.

Emergency power

Some of us take a break to get away from our mobile (cell) phones, but for those who can't leave home without them, you need never worry about a flat battery again: Eurohike have an ingenious solution: a wind-up torch with a mobile phone charger attached. Available from **www.millets.co.uk**.

Register at the embassy

If you're travelling to a high risk country where security is an issue, it's a good idea (and sometimes mandatory) to register at your embassy as soon as you arrive so you can be accounted for if anything happens. Similarly, if you lose everything on holiday – bags, passport, the lot – you should contact your embassy or consular services immediately to obtain temporary travel documentation and emergency cash.

Help, I'm lost!

If you are going to spend any time in a remote area on your next holiday, take your mobile (cell) phone with you. Sounds counter-intuitive when you can't always get reception in your home town, but they have saved a number of stranded travellers from life threatening predicaments.

The intrepid explorer

When you venture into the wild, always tell someone where you're going and when you expect to be back – even if it's just the receptionist at the hotel. That way, if you get lost and find yourself in need of rescue, the emergency services can always trace your steps.

The less intrepid explorer

For the less intrepid explorers out there, always remember to get a business card from your hotel and take it with you whenever you venture out. The address could come in handy if you find yourself lost in an unknown part of town.

Live to tell the tale

If you find yourself lost in a remote area and facing an emergency, don't panic. Just stay where you are and wait for someone to find you. If you've told someone where you are going, this shouldn't take long. First find shelter, then think about where you can get water and food.

Take a carabiner

If you've never been rock climbing you may not have encountered a carabiner before but they are an excellent travel security item. It is a metal loop with a sprung or screwed gate and is the quickest, safest way to make sure your bags don't get snatched. In a train station restaurant, for example, use a carabiner to attach the straps of your bags to the table leg so if someone tries to make a grab-and-dash, they'll end up taking the furniture and ketchup with them as well.

Top 10

farthest reaches of the World

1 The closest point on earth to the sun is an extinct volcano on the equator in Ecuador, known as Chimborazo, rising 6267 metres above sea level.

2 The lowest point on earth is the Dead Sea in the Middle East, 400 metres below sea level.

3 The wettest place in the world is Mawsynram in India which gets a staggering 12 metres of rainfall every year.

4 The driest place in the world is the Atacama Desert in Chile which, on average, receives less than a millimetre of rain a year.

5 The world's largest living structure is the 2000 kilometre Great Barrier Reef off the north east coast of Australia.

6 The world's most remote inhabited place is Easter Island, 4000 kilometres off the west coast of South America.

7   The world's oldest rainforest is the 130 million-year-old Taman Negara near Kuala Lumpur in Malaysia.

8   The world's most recently discovered species of mammal is the Muntjac Deer, found in Vietnam in 1994.

9   The largest festival in the world is India's Kumbha Mela which attracts over 10 million people.

10 The world's longest river is the 6680 kilometre Nile in Africa, but the world's largest river is the Amazon in South America, which holds a fifth of the entire world's fresh water.

Travel Checklist

Apart from the necessary clothing and toiletries and depending on your trip, the following list will prove useful ...

- Valid passport
- Valid visa (if required)
- Travel tickets and itinerary
- Travel company contact details
- Travel insurance details
- Accommodation booking details / reference numbers
- Driving licence
- Car rental booking details / reference number
- Phrase book and a few sheets of notes on the places you want to visit. (Don't take the whole travel guide with you – read it before you travel!)
- Notebook, pen and calculator
- Cash (your currency and that of destination)
- Traveller's cheques
- Credit card
- Money belt
- Luggage labels (outward and return)
- Camera (with films or data card) and mini camera tripod
- Video camera with films if you must! Remember – it can pack a lot of weight
- Charged and/or spare batteries for cameras
- Electrical adapters appropriate for destination

- Binoculars
- Torch with new batteries (a head torch is preferable)
- Travel alarm clock
- Travel sickness pills
- A good book
- Sunglasses
- Sun screen and after sun / sunburn lotion
- Salt replacement sachets
- Water purifying tablets
- Carbohydrate snacks (in case of travel delays)
- Mirror
- Sewing kit and safety pins
- Basic first aid items including aloe vera gel
- Insect repellent spray or lotion and insect bite cream
- Mosquito net
- Eye shades and ear plugs
- Sarong
- Flip flops
- Travel towel (very absorbent)
- Wet wipes
- Re-sealable or zip-lock sandwich bags
- Backpack rain cover and waterproof stuff sack

- Duct tape (fixes everything!)
- Fishing line (strongest string in the world!)
- Swiss Army knife or Leatherman tool (packed in case NOT hand luggage)

Also remember to ...

- Have inoculations if required (arrange these in plenty of time).
- Buy sufficient insurance for your trip.
- Let relatives know how to contact you in case of emergency.
- Tell friends / neighbours the length of your absence.
- Arrange for care of pets in your absence.
- Cancel milk, newspaper and other regular deliveries but NOT by doorstep note.
- Not leave a message on your answerphone saying how long you are away for.
- Switch off electrical appliances and make sure no taps are left running.
- Leave something in the freezer to cook when you get back.
- Arrange for a friend to check on your house whilst you are away.
- Book a taxi (if you need one) to take you to the airport, or book your parking space (cheaper when booked in advance).
- Brush up on your local knowledge of the place you will be visiting.

> Like all great travellers, I have seen more than I remember, and remember more than I have seen.

Benjamin Disraeli

Top 20

cultural tips

1. In France, don't bring a bottle. Supplying the wine for a dinner party can imply that their own is not up to scratch.

2. South Korean food can be spicy but even if your nose runs, resist the temptation to wipe it! Using a handkerchief at the table is not polite.

3. In Pakistan, the left hand is reserved for the toilet so whenever paying someone or passing something to them, always use your right. This applies to food as well so unless you enjoy eating alone, never put food into your mouth with your left hand.

4. In Brazil, Turkey, and Russia the OK sign (made with the thumb and index finger) is an obscenity and, unless you're looking for trouble, is best avoided.

5. In Bangladesh it's frowned upon for men and women to show affection in public but perfectly normal to see two men walking down the street holding hands.

6 In Muslim countries you should always take your shoes off when visiting mosques and people's houses. It also shows respect to keep your shoulders and knees covered in public. Women might also need a headscarf.

7 When giving flowers in Vietnam you should always give an even number, while in Bulgaria you should always give an odd number.

8 In many parts of the Middle East and Asia, the soles of the feet are taboo and should not be seen, shown, or touched at any point.

9 In China, gifts are an important part of the culture but never give a clock as a present. Rather than being an attractive addition to the mantelpiece, it suggests you are counting the hours until the recipient's death.

10 In Japan, death is represented by the colour white so you should avoid giving gifts that are wrapped in white paper.

11 In Laos don't be surprised when you see men with long, manicured fingernails as they are very fashionable.

12 Throughout Asia, you will find you get a lot further when you keep your cool. If something is taking longer than expected, do not show your frustration as many cultures see this as 'losing face' and you will not be regarded with the same respect.

13 In South America, gesturing for someone to 'come here' by curling your fingers and palm towards your body is sexually suggestive and should be reserved for more private moments.

14 Never point with your finger in Indonesia – it's a rude gesture. Use your thumb instead.

15 In Greece, waving an open-palmed hand at someone to greet them can be offensive so it is best to keep your palm closed or facing in towards your body.

16 In Buddhist culture, the head is the most sacred part of the body and can only be touched by a close member of the family; never by a stranger.

17 In Thailand it's not a good idea to step on a bank note or even lick a postage stamp as both bear the King's head and this is a sign of disrespect.

18 In some remote parts of South East Asia countries, the camera lens is thought to capture a piece of the soul so you should always ask permission or offer payment before taking a photo and receiving this gift from people.

19 In Italy, you should never enter a church wearing shorts, a short skirt, or a vest. Your legs and upper arms should always be covered as a mark of respect.

20 In India, always get directions from several people as it can be considered more impolite to admit you do not know the answer than it is to give an incorrect answer.

Country Facts

Country	Capital	Official language	Currency	Time Zone
Australia	Canberra	English	Australian dollars	+8 to +10
Bahamas	Nassau	English	Bahamian dollar	-5
Belize	Belmopan	English	Belizean dollar	-6
Bolivia	La Paz	Spanish	Boliviano	-4
Brazil	Brasilia	Portuguese	Real	-3 to -4
Cambodia	Phnom Penh	Khmer	Riel	+7
Canada	Ottawa	English/ French	Canadian dollars	-4 to -9
Chile	Santiago	Spanish	Chilean peso	-4
China	Beijing	Mandarin	Yuan	+8
Costa Rica	San Jose	Spanish	Costa Rican colon	-6
Croatia	Zagreb	Croatian	Kuna	+1

	Why visit?
	Australia has some of the most unique wildlife, landscapes and indigenous culture in the world.
	Of 700 Bahamian islands, only 30 are inhabited.
	In a world where old growth rainforest is in rapid decline, two thirds of the original Belizean rainforest remains.
	Bolivia is a country of other worldly landscapes, none less so than the Altiplano salt flats; 4,000 metres up in the Andean mountains.
	Larger than the United States, Brazil has everything from cosmopolitan cities to ecology still unknown to man.
	The Ankor Wat temple complex in Cambodia is one of the architectural wonders of the world; partly submerged in the tangled roots of banyan trees.
	Canada is the world's second largest country with laid back cities, wild back country and great skiing.
	Over just a few hundred kilometres in Chile you can travel from the coast to the desert to snow capped Andean mountains.
	China is home to the world's oldest surviving civilisation, which invented the abacas, the compass, and the earliest printing techniques.
	Costa Rica is Central America's most accessible destination with jungle-fringed beaches and striking ecological diversity.
	Croatia's Adriatic islands offer some of the best sailing in the world.

Country	Capital	Official language	Currency	Time Zone
Cuba	Havana	Spanish	Cuban peso	-5
Czech Republic	Prague	Czech	Czech koruna	+1
Ecuador	Quito	Spanish	US dollar	-5
Egypt	Cairo	Arabic	Egyptian pound	+2
Estonia	Tallinn	Estonian	Kroon	+2
Fiji	Suva	Fijian	Fiji dollar	+12
France	Paris	French	Euro	+1
Germany	Berlin	German	Euro	+1
Greece	Athens	Greek	Euro	+2
Honduras	Tegucigalpa	Spanish	Lempira	-6
Iceland	Reykjavik	Icelandic	Icelandic krona	GMT

Why visit?
Cuban music is legendary and the Caribbean's largest island will open your eyes to a completely different way of life.
The Czech Republic is a timeless destination famed for its cobbled backstreets and bohemian culture.
Ecuador's primeval landscape is home to some of the world's most important ecosystems.
The great pyramids of Egypt are testimony to one of history's greatest civilisations.
In Estonia you can enjoy medieval architecture by day and lively bars by night.
Built on a series of extinct volcanoes that rise from the ocean floor, Fijian culture and customs have remained unchanged for generations.
Go to France to indulge in some of the world's best food and wine.
From Einstein to Goethe, Germany is the birthplace of some of the world's greatest minds.
Best known for its Mediterranean islands, Greece is also recognised as the birthplace of Western civilisation.
The Bay Islands, off the north coast of Honduras, are the cheapest place in the world to learn to scuba dive.
Iceland is an isolated volcanic retreat in the North Atlantic where you can enjoy whale watching and white water rafting.

Country	Capital	Official language	Currency	Time Zone
India	New Delhi	Hindi	Indian rupees	+5½
Indonesia	Jakarta	Bahasa	Indonesia rupiah	+7 to +9
Ireland	Dublin	English	Euro	GMT
Italy	Rome	Italian	Euro	+1
Jamaica	Kingston	English	Jamaican dollar	-5
Japan	Tokyo	Japanese	Yen	+9
Jordan	Amman	Arabic	Jordanian dinar	+2
Kenya	Nairobi	Kiswahili	Kenya shilling	+3
Madagascar	Antananarivo	Malagasy	Malagasy franc	+3
Malawi	Lilongwe	English	Malawian kwacha	+2
Malaysia	Kuala Lumpur	English	Ringgit	+8
Mauritius	Port Louis	English / French	Mauritian rupee	+4

	Why visit?
	Home to a rich variety of culture, India is one of the cheapest travel destinations going.
	In Indonesia you'll find great food, ancient heritage, exotic wildlife and 10% of the world's remaining tropical rainforest.
	Ireland's wild coastline, lively pubs and welcoming hosts make it a first class destination.
	Italian art and music have influenced global culture for hundreds of years.
	Home to one of the world's most influential styles of popular music, the reggae-infused island of Jamaica also grows some of the world's best coffee.
	Japan is a curious mix of frenetic cities and gentle cultural traditions.
	In Jordan you'll find the enigmatic 'lost' city of Petra, hand-cut from the arid, rocky landscape.
	A wildlife safari in Kenya is made all the more spectacular by the Great Rift Valley backdrop.
	On the world's fourth largest island, every native mammal in Madagascar is endemic.
	Malawi is one of Africa's most compact, accessible and varied destinations.
	Parts of the Malaysian rainforest are older than any other in the world.
	Mauritius was described by Mark Twain as being a blueprint for heaven.

Country	Capital	Official language	Currency	TIme Zone
Mexico	Mexico City	Spanish	Mexican peso	-6
Morocco	Rabat	Arabic	Moroccan dirham	GMT
Mozambique	Maputo	Portuguese	Metical	+2
Nepal	Kathmandu	Nepalese	Nepalese rupee	+5¾
New Zealand	Wellington	English	New Zealand dollars	+12
Norway	Oslo	Norwegian	Norwegian krone	+1
Peru	Lima	Spanish	New sol	-5
Seychelles	Victoria	English/ French	Seychelles rupee	+4
South Africa	Pretoria	Afrikaans	Rand	+2
Spain	Madrid	Spanish	Euro	+1
Sri Lanka	Colombo	Sinhala/ Tamil	Sri Lankan rupee	+6

Why visit?
The Mayan and Aztec temples of Mexico were built by two of history's most dynamic civilisations.
In Morocco you'll find a heady mix of bustling marketplaces, rugged mountains, and intricate Islamic architecture.
For isolated, stunning and accessible beaches, head to the coast of Mozambique.
Nepal is home to eight of the world's ten highest peaks, walked by the hardy Gurkhas and Sherpas for generations.
New Zealand is an adventure sports playground maturing into one of the world's top wine producers.
The Norwegian wilderness runs right down to its dramatic fjord-cut coastline, while its capital brims with art, music and culture.
Peru is one of the most environmentally diverse countries in the world, where you'll also find the famous Incan city of Machu Pichu.
The Seychelles are 115 coral islands surrounded by clear, calm seas.
South Africa is an accessible destination where you can enjoy as much wildlife in the city as you can in the national parks.
Spain has many attributes but the highlight is Barcelona: acknowledged as one of the best cities in the world.
The tropical, bitesize island of Sri Lanka is a good destination for families and independent travellers.

Country	Capital	Official language	Currency	Time Zone
Switzerland	Bern	German	Swiss francs	+1
Tanzania	Dodoma	English	Tanzanian shilling	+3
Thailand	Bangkok	Thai	Baht	+7
Turkey	Ankara	Turkish	Turkish lira	+2
United Kingdom	London	English	Pound sterling	GMT
United States	Washington DC	English	American dollars	-5 to -8
Vietnam	Hanoi	Vietnamese	Dong	+7

Why visit?
Sedate travellers in Switzerland enjoy the picturesque cities and refined culture while the adrenalin-hunters hit the action in the Alps.
Tanzania's ethnic diversity is magnificent, as is Kilimanjaro: the highest peak in Africa.
Thailand is an easy going destination with an open culture, great food and fantastic beaches.
Turkey is often noted as a confluence of continents and for good reason: it is a fascinating slice of life.
The U.K. is a historian's treasure chest with relaxing countryside retreats and influential urban culture.
The U.S. caters for every travel taste with remote of America environments and glamorous, fast-paced cities.
Vietnam is an inexpensive place to enjoy world heritage environments and great ethnic diversity.

International Clothing Sizes

Men

SUITS, COATS & SWEATERS

US	36	38	40	42	44	46
UK	36	38	40	42	44	46
European	46	48	51	54	56	59

SHIRTS

US	14	14½	15	15½	16	16½	17
UK	14	14½	15	15½	16	16½	17
European	36	37	38	39	41	42	43

SHOES

US	7½	8	8½	9½	10½	11½
UK	7	7½	8	9	10	11
European	40½	41	42	43	44½	46

SOCKS

US	9½	10	10½	11	11½	12
UK	9½	10	10½	11	11½	12
European	39	40	41	42	43	44

HATS

US	$6^5/_8$	$6¾$	$6^7/_8$	7	$7^1/_8$	7¼	$7^3/_8$	7½
UK	6½	$6^5/_8$	6¾	$6^7/_8$	7	$7^1/_8$	7¼	$7^3/_8$
European	53	54	55	56	57	58	59	60

Women

SUITS, COATS & SWEATERS

US	8	10	12	14	16	18
UK	10	12	14	16	18	20
European	38	40	42	44	46	48

BLOUSES & SWEATERS

US	34	36	38	40	42	44
UK	36	38	40	42	44	46
European	42	44	46	48	50	52

SHOES

US	6	6½	7	7½	8	8½
UK	4½	5	5½	6	6½	7
European	37½	38	39	39½	40	40½

Children

US	4	6	8	10	12	14
UK (Ht inches)	43	48	55	58	60	62
European (Ht cm)	109	122	140	147	152	157

Temperature conversions

Celsius °C	Fahrenheit °F	Celsius °C	Fahrenheit °F
-30°C	-22°F	16°C	60.8°F
-20°C	-4.0°F	17°C	62.6°F
-10°C	14.0°F	18°C	64.4°F
0°C	32.0°F	19°C	66.2°F
1°C	33.8°F	20°C	68.0°F
2°C	35.6°F	21°C	69.8°F
3°C	37.4°F	22°C	71.6°F
4°C	39.2°F	23°C	73.4°F
5°C	41.0°F	24°C	75.2°F
6°C	42.8°F	25°C	77.0°F
7°C	44.6°F	26°C	78.8°F
8°C	46.4°F	27°C	80.6°F
9°C	48.2°F	28°C	82.4°F
10°C	50.0°F	29°C	84.2°F
11°C	51.8°F	30°C	86.0°F
12°C	53.6°F	40°C	104°F
13°C	55.4°F	50°C	122°F
14°C	57.2°F	60°C	140°F
15°C	59.0°F		

To convert Fahrenheit to Centigrade: $C = \frac{5}{9} \times (F-32)$
To convert Centigrade to Fahrenheit: $F = (\frac{9}{5} \times C) + 32$

My tips

Index

'The Greatest Tips in the World' books

Baby & Toddler Tips
by Vicky Burford
ISBN 978-1-905151-70-7

Barbeque Tips
by Raymond van Rijk
ISBN 978-1-905151-68-4

Cat Tips by Joe Inglis
ISBN 978-1-905151-66-0

Cookery Tips
by Peter Osborne
ISBN 978-1-905151-64-6

Cricketing Tips
by R. Rotherham & G. Clifford
ISBN 978-1-905151-18-9

DIY Tips
by Chris Jones & Brian Lee
ISBN 978-1-905151-62-2

Dog Tips by Joe Inglis
ISBN 978-1-905151-67-7

Etiquette & Dining Tips
by Prof. R. Rotherham
ISBN 978-1-905151-21-9

Freelance Writing Tips
by Linda Jones
ISBN 978-1-905151-17-2

Gardening Tips
by Steve Brookes
ISBN 978-1-905151-60-8

Genealogy Tips
by M. Vincent-Northam
ISBN 978-1-905151-72-1

Golfing Tips
by John Cook
ISBN 978-1-905151-63-9

Horse & Pony Tips
by Joanne Bednall
ISBN 978-1-905151-19-6

Household Tips
by Vicky Burford
ISBN 978-1-905151-61-5

Personal Success Tips
by Brian Larcher
ISBN 978-1-905151-71-4

Podcasting Tips
by Malcolm Boyden
ISBN 978-1-905151-75-2

Property Developing Tips
by F. Morgan & P Morgan
ISBN 978-1-905151-69-1

Retirement Tips
by Tony Rossiter
ISBN 978-1-905151-28-8

Sex Tips
by Julie Peasgood
ISBN 978-1-905151-74-5

Travel Tips
by Simon Worsfold
ISBN 978-1-905151-73-8

Yoga Tips
by D. Gellineau & D. Robson
ISBN 978-1-905151-65-3

Pet Recipe books

The Greatest Feline Feasts in the World by Joe Inglis
ISBN 978-1-905151-50-9

The Greatest Doggie Dinners in the World by Joe Inglis
ISBN 978-1-905151-51-6

'The Greatest in the World' DVDs

The Greatest in the World – Gardening Tips
presented by Steve Brookes

The Greatest in the World – Yoga Tips
presented by David Gellineau and David Robson

The Greatest in the World – Cat & Kitten Tips
presented by Joe Inglis

The Greatest in the World – Dog & Puppy Tips
presented by Joe Inglis

For more information about currently available
and forthcoming book and DVD titles please visit:

www.thegreatestintheworld.com

or write to:

The Greatest in the World Ltd
PO Box 3182
Stratford-upon-Avon
Warwickshire CV37 7XW
United Kingdom

Tel / Fax: +44(0)1789 299616
Email: info@thegreatestintheworld.com

The author

Growing up in Britain in the eighties, the author was fortunate enough to travel all over the world at a young age: spending his winters skiing and his summers wherever the sun shone better than home.

As soon as he was old enough to go it alone, he branched out and ventured further afield to India, Nepal and southern Africa before settling into two years working for a travel company that sends volunteers to work on projects around the world. This only aggravated the travel bug and before long he left with his American girlfriend (who he later married) to spend a year in Australia and South East Asia. From here he wrote a regular travel advice column for Verge magazine, based in Canada.

After all this, aged twenty eight, he still says there's nothing quite as exciting as the feeling of being pressed into the back of an airline seat when the pilot puts the throttle down for take off, and with close family in both Australia and the United States, this looks set to continue.